Additional praise for *Credit Risk Scorecards*...

"An essential book for anyone interested in retail credit risk modeling. Written by an experienced credit scoring practitioner, it provides a unique and comprehensive insight into the scorecard development process."

—Nor Zihan Ismail,
Credit Risk Analytics Specialist,
Malaysian leading bank

Credit Risk Scorecards

Developing and Implementing Intelligent Credit Scoring

NAEEM SIDDIQI

WILEY

John Wiley & Sons, Inc.

Published by John Wiley & Sons, Inc., Hoboken, New Jersey.

Published simultaneously in Canada.

For general information on our other products and services, or technical support, please contact our Customer Care Department within the United States at 800–762–2974, outside the United States at 317–572–3993 or fax 317–572–4002.

Wiley also publishes its books in a variety of electronic formats. Some content that appears in print may not be available in electronic books.

For more information about Wiley products, visit our Web site at http://www.wiley.com.

SAS and all other SAS Institute Inc. product or service names are registered trademarks or trademarks of SAS Institute Inc. in the USA and other countries. (r) indicates USA registration.

Library of Congress Cataloging-in-Publication Data:

Siddiqi, Naeem, 1969–
   Credit risk scorecards: developing and implementing intelligent credit scoring / Naeem Siddiqi.
      p. cm.
   Includes bibliographical references and index.
   ISBN-13: 978–0–471–75451–0 (cloth)
   ISBN-10: 0–471–75451-X (cloth)
      1. Credit scoring systems.   2. Risk management.   I. Title.
HG3751.5.S53 2006
658.8'8—dc22
                                    2005017415

Printed in the United States of America

10   9   8   7   6   5

To Noor and Zainab, for giving me unparalleled joy.

Contents

Acknowledgments

Writing a good book, like developing a good scorecard, is never a one-person show. I would like to express my gratitude to a few people who have supported me in this endeavor.

I would like to thank:

- Dr. David Yeo, Hendrik Wagner, and Clark Abrahams of SAS, for their invaluable suggestions on, and contributions to, the content of this book.
- Lorne Rothman and John Amrhein of SAS Canada for helping to enhance my knowledge of data mining.
- Stephenie Joyner of SAS Publishing, for her patience and perseverance.

I want to thank my family—Saleha, Zainab, and Noor—for tolerating my frequent absences from home, and the hours spent in my office working on the book.

Finally I want to acknowledge my parents for encouraging me to seek knowledge, and for their constant prayers and blessings, without which there would be no success.

CHAPTER 1

Introduction

Increased competition and growing pressures for revenue generation have led credit-granting and other financial institutions to search for more effective ways to attract new creditworthy customers, and at the same time, control losses. Aggressive marketing efforts have resulted in deeper penetration of the risk pool of potential customers, and the need to process them rapidly and effectively has led to growing automation of the credit and insurance application and adjudication processes. The Risk Manager is now challenged to produce risk adjudication solutions that can not only satisfactorily assess creditworthiness, but also keep the per-unit processing cost low, while reducing turnaround times for customers. In addition, customer service excellence demands that this automated process be able to minimize denial of credit to creditworthy customers, while keeping out as many potentially delinquent ones as possible. In the insurance sector, the ability to keep the prices of policies commensurate with claims risk becomes more critical as underwriting losses increase across the industry.

At the customer management level, companies are striving ever harder to keep their existing clients by offering them additional products and enhanced services. Risk Managers are called on to help in selecting the "right" (i.e., low risk) customers for these favored treatments. Conversely, for customers who exhibit negative behavior (non-payment, fraud), Risk Managers need to devise strategies to not only identify them, but also deal with them effectively to minimize further loss and recoup any monies owed, as quickly as possible.

It is in this environment that risk scorecards offer a powerful, empirically derived solution to business needs. Risk scorecards have been used by a variety of industries for uses including predicting delinquency nonpayment—that is, bankruptcy—fraud, claims (for insurance), and recovery of amounts owed for accounts in collections. Scoring methodology offers an objective way to assess risk, and also a consistent approach, provided that system overrides are kept to a minimum.

In the past, financial institutions acquired credit risk scorecards from a handful of credit risk vendors. This involved the financial institution providing their data to the vendors, and the vendors then developing a predictive scorecard for delivery. While some advanced companies have had internal modeling and scorecard development functions for a long time, the trend toward developing scorecards in-house has become far more widespread in the last few years. This happened for various reasons.

First, application software became available that allowed users to develop scorecards without investing heavily in advanced programmers and infrastructure. Complex data mining functions became available at the click of a mouse, allowing the user to spend more time applying business and data mining expertise to the problem, rather than debugging complicated programs. The availability of powerful "point and click"–based Extract-Transform-Load (ETL) software enabled efficient extraction and preparation of data for scorecard development and other data mining. Second, advances in intelligent and easy to access data storage have removed much of the burden of gathering the required data and putting it into a form that is amenable to analysis.

Once the tools became available, in-house development became a viable option for many smaller and medium-sized institutions. The industry could now realize the significant Return on Investment (ROI) that in-house scorecard development could deliver for the right players. Experience has shown that in-house credit scorecard development can be done faster, cheaper, and with far more flexibility than before. Development was cheaper, since the cost of maintaining an in-house credit scoring capability was less than the cost of purchased scorecards. Internal development capability also allowed companies to develop far more scorecards (with enhanced segmentation) for the same expenditure. Scorecards could also be developed faster by internal resources using the right software—which meant that custom scorecards could be implemented faster, leading to lower losses.

In addition, companies realized that their superior knowledge of internal data and business insights led them to develop better-performing scorecards. Defining the population performance definitions is a critical part of scoring system construction, and the ability to vary definitions for different purposes is key. For example, a probability of default score designed for capital planning purposes may exclude moderately delinquent accounts (60 days past due twice during the past 24 months) that are normally included in "bad behavior" and go by the Basel definition for loans considered likely to default (associated with write-off, repossession, foreclosure, judgments, or bankruptcy). This will vary by type of loan or trade line—for example, revolving, installment, mortgage, and so forth. On sample construction, some Scorecard Developers eliminate large numbers of accounts associated with inactivity, indeterminate behavior, and so forth, and this is another area where some empirical investigation and control is warranted.

Better-performing scorecards also came about from having the flexibility to experiment with segmentation, and from following through by developing the optimum number and configuration of scorecards.

Internal scorecard development also increases the knowledge base within organizations. The analyses done reveal hidden treasures of information that allow for better understanding of customers' risk behavior, and lead to better strategy development.

In summary, leaving key modeling and sampling decisions to "external experts" can prove to be a suboptimal route at best, and can also be quite costly. A perfect example that comes to mind is a finance company that outsourced scorecard development and found upon system implementation that the "updated scorecards" turned down 65% of their current and repeat customers, even though they developed specific individual scorecards for present versus former borrowers. Ultimately, the problem was traced back to the good/bad performance definitions and the fact that their average "good" paying customer had delinquency characteristics that would normally be categorized as bad behavior, or indeterminate at the very least! Unfortunately, there were five regional scorecards for each of the two groups, so that ultimately ten scorecards were shelved at an average cost of $27,000. There was also fallout with customers who were initially turned down after 20 years of doing business with the company.

This book presents a business-focused process for the development and implementation of risk prediction scorecards, one that builds upon a solid foundation of statistics and data mining principles. Statistical and data mining techniques and methodologies have been discussed in detail in various publications, and will not be covered in depth here. The key concepts that will be covered are:

- The application of business intelligence to the scorecard development process, so that the development and implementation of scorecards is seen as an intelligent business solution to a business problem. Good scorecards are not built by passing data solely through a series of programs or algorithms—they are built when the data is passed through the analytical and business-trained mind of the user.

- Collaborative scorecard development, in which end users, subject matter experts, implementers, modelers, and other stakeholders work in a cohesive and coherent manner to get better results.

- The concept of building a risk profile—building scorecards that contain predictive variables representing major information categories. This mimics the thought processes of good risk adjudicators, who analyze information from credit applications, or customer behavior, and create a profile based on the different types of information available. They would not make a decision using four or five pieces of information only—so why should anyone build a scorecard that is narrow-based?

- Anticipating impacts of decisions and preparing for them. Each decision made—whether on the definition of the target variable, segmentation, choice of variables, transformations, choice of cutoffs, or other strategies—starts a chain of events that impacts other areas of the company, as well as future performance. By tapping into corporate intelligence, and working in collaboration with others, the user will learn to anticipate the impact of each decision and prepare accordingly to minimize disruption and unpleasant surprises.

- View of scorecards as decision support tools. Scorecards should be viewed as a tool to be used for better decision making, and should be created with this view. This means they must be understood and controlled; scorecard development should not result in a complex model that cannot be understood enough to make decisions or perform diagnostics.

Individual scorecard development projects may need to be dealt with differently, depending on each company's unique situation. This methodology should therefore be viewed as a set of guidelines rather than as a set of definitive rules that must be followed. Finally, it is worth noting that regulatory compliance plays an important part in ensuring that scorecards used for granting consumer credit are statistically sound, empirically derived, and capable of separating creditworthy from noncreditworthy applicants at a statistically significant rate.[1] An excellent, but somewhat dated, article on credit scoring and the Equal Credit Opportunity Act is cited in the Bibliography (Hsia, 1978).

SCORECARDS: GENERAL OVERVIEW

Risk scoring, as with other predictive models, is a tool used to evaluate the level of risk associated with applicants or customers. While it does not identify "good" (no negative behavior expected) or "bad" (negative behavior expected) applications on an individual basis, it provides statistical odds, or probability, that an applicant with any given score will be "good" or "bad." These probabilities or scores, along with other business considerations such as expected approval rates, profit, churn, and losses, are then used as a basis for decision making.

In its simplest form, a scorecard consists of a group of characteristics, statistically determined to be predictive in separating good and bad accounts. For reference, Exhibit 1.1 shows a part of a scorecard.

EXHIBIT 1.1   SAMPLE SCORECARD (PARTIAL)

Characteristic Name	Attribute	Scorecard Points
AGE	-> 23	63
AGE	23 -> 25	76
AGE	25 -> 28	79
AGE	28 -> 34	85
AGE	34 -> 46	94
AGE	46 -> 51	103
AGE	51 ->	105
CARDS	"AMERICAN EXPRESS," "VISA OTHERS," "VISA MYBANK," "NO CREDIT CARDS"	80
CARDS	"CHEQUE CARD," "MASTERCARD/EUROC," "OTHER CREDIT CARD"	99
EC_CARD	0	86
EC_CARD	1	83
INCOME	-> 500	93
INCOME	500 -> 1,550	81
INCOME	1,550 -> 1,850	75
INCOME	1,850 -> 2,550	80
INCOME	2,550 ->	88
STATUS	"E," "T," "U"	79

Scorecard characteristics may be selected from any of the sources of data available to the lender at the time of the application. Examples of such characteristics are demographics (e.g., age, time at residence, time at job, postal code), existing relationship (e.g., time at bank, number of products, payment performance, previous claims), credit bureau (e.g., inquiries, trades, delinquency, public records), real estate data, and so forth.

Each attribute ("Age" is a *characteristic* and "23–25" is an *attribute*) is assigned points based on statistical analyses, taking into consideration various factors such as the predictive strength of the characteristics, correlation between characteristics, and operational factors. The total score of an applicant is the sum of the scores for each attribute present in the scorecard for that applicant.

Exhibit 1.2 is an example of one of the management reports produced during scorecard development.

The circled line in the exhibit tells us the following:

EXHIBIT 1.2   GAINS CHART

Score Range	Count	Cumulative Count	Number of Goods	Cumulative Number of Goods	Number of Bads	Cumulative Number of Bads	Marginal Badrate	Cumulative Badrate	Approval Rate
273 <= Score <279	842	842	840	840	2	2	0.24	0.24	1.81
267 <= Score <273	511	1,353	510	1,350	1	3	0.20	0.22	2.91
262 <= Score <267	574	1,927	570	1,920	4	7	0.70	0.36	4.14
256 <= Score <262	2,087	4,014	2,070	3,990	17	24	0.81	0.60	8.63
250 <= Score <256	1,756	5,770	1,740	5,730	16	40	0.91	0.69	12.41
245 <= Score <250	2,339	8,109	2,310	8,040	28	68	1.20	0.84	17.44
239 <= Score <245	2,917	11,026	2,880	10,920	37	105	1.27	0.95	23.71
233 <= Score <239	3,774	14,799	3,720	14,640	54	159	1.43	1.07	31.83
228 <= Score <233	2,766	17,565	2,700	17,340	66	225	2.39	1.28	37.77
222 <= Score <228	3,366	20,931	3,300	20,640	66	291	1.96	1.39	45.01
216 <= Score <222	4,492	25,423	4,380	25,020	112	403	2.49	1.59	54.67
211 <= Score <216	4,210	29,633	4,080	29,100	130	533	3.09	1.80	63.73
205 <= Score <211	3,455	33,088	3,360	32,460	95	628	2.75	1.90	71.16
199 <= Score <205	4,419	37,507	4,260	36,720	159	787	3.60	2.10	80.66
194 <= Score <199	1,549	39,056	1,440	38,160	109	896	7.04	2.29	83.99
188 <= Score <194	2,006	41,062	1,890	40,050	116	1,012	5.78	2.46	88.31

- For the score range 245–250, the expected marginal bad rate is 1.2%. That is, 1.2% of applicants with a score between 245 and 250 will likely be "bad."
- The cumulative bad rate—that is, the bad rate of all applicants above 245—is 0.84%.
- The acceptance rate at 245 is 17.44%, that is, 17.44% of all applicants score above 245.

Based on factors outlined above, a company can then decide, for example, to decline all applicants who score below 200, or to charge them higher pricing in view of the greater risk they present. "Bad" is generally defined using negative performance indicators such as bankruptcy, fraud, delinquency, write-off/chargeoff, and negative net present value (NPV).

Risk score information, combined with other factors such as expected approval rate and revenue/profit potential at each risk level, can be used to develop new application strategies that will maximize revenue and minimize bad debt. Some of the strategies for high-risk applicants are:

- Declining credit/services if the risk level is too high
- Assigning a lower starting credit limit on a credit card or line of credit
- Asking the applicant to provide a higher down payment or deposit for mortgages or car loans
- Charging a higher interest rate on a loan
- Charging a higher premium on insurance policies
- Asking the applicant to provide a deposit for utilities services
- Offering prepaid cellular services instead of postpaid
- Denying international calling access from telecommunications companies
- Putting the applicant into a "watch list" for potential fraudulent activity

Conversely, high-scoring applicants may be given preferential rates and higher credit limits, and be offered upgrades to premium products, such as gold or platinum cards, or additional products offered by the company.

Application scores can also help in setting "due diligence" policies. For example, an applicant scoring very high or very low can be declined or approved outright without obtaining further information on real estate, income verification, or valuation of underlying security.

The previous examples specifically dealt with risk scoring at the application stage. Risk scoring is similarly used with existing clients on an ongoing basis. In this context, the client's behavioral data with the company is used to predict the probability of negative behavior. Based on similar business considerations as previously mentioned (e.g., expected risk and profitability levels), different treatments can be tailored to accounts, such as:

- Offering product upgrades and additional products
- Increasing credit limits on credit cards and lines of credit

- Allowing some revolving credit customers to go beyond their credit limits
- Flagging potentially fraudulent transactions
- Offering better pricing on loan/insurance policy renewals
- Deciding whether or not to reissue an expired credit card
- Prequalifying direct marketing lists for cross-selling
- Directing delinquent accounts to more stringent collection methods or outsourcing to a collection agency
- Suspending or revoking phone services or credit facilities
- Put an account into a "watch list" for potential fraudulent activity

In addition to being developed for use with new applicants (application scoring) or existing accounts (behavior scoring), scorecards can also be defined based on the type of data used to develop them. Custom scorecards are those developed using data for customers of one organization exclusively. For example, ABC Bank uses the performance data of its own customers to build a scorecard to predict bankruptcy. It may use internal data or data obtained from a credit bureau for this purpose, but the data is only for its own customers.

Generic or pooled data scorecards are those built using data from multiple lenders. For example, four small banks, none of which has enough data to build its own custom scorecards, decide to pool their data for auto loans. They then build a scorecard with this data and share it, or customize the scorecards based on unique characteristics of their portfolios. Scorecards built using industry bureau data, and marketed by credit bureaus, are a type of generic scorecards.

Risk scoring, in addition to being a tool to evaluate levels of risk, has also been effectively applied in other operational areas, such as:

- Streamlining the decision-making process, that is, higher-risk and borderline applications being given to more experienced staff for more scrutiny, while low-risk applications are assigned to junior staff. This can be done in branches, credit adjudication centers, and collections departments.

- Reducing turnaround time for processing applications through automated decision making
- Evaluating quality of portfolios intended for acquisition
- Setting economic and regulatory capital allocation
- Setting pricing for securitization of receivables portfolios
- Comparing the quality of business from different channels/regions/ suppliers

Risk scoring, therefore, provides creditors with an opportunity for consistent and objective decision making, based on empirically derived information. Combined with business knowledge, predictive modeling technologies provide risk managers with added efficiency and control over the risk management process.

In the future, credit scoring is expected to play an enhanced role in large banking organizations, due to the requirements of the new Basel Capital Accord (Basel II). This will also lead to a reevaluation of methodologies and strategy development for scorecards, based on the recommendations of the final accord. In particular, changes may be required in the way "bad" is defined, and in the way the target prediction is connected to "Probability of Default," "Exposure at Default," and "Loss Given Default."

ENDNOTE

1. Regulation B, Section 202.2(p) (1) (i–iv).

CHAPTER 2

Scorecard Development: The People and the Process

The process of scorecard development needs to be a collaborative one between information technology (IT), data mining, and operational staff. This not only creates better scorecards, it ensures that the solutions are consistent with business direction, and enables education and knowledge transfer during the development process. Scorecard development is not a "black box" process, and should not be treated as such. Experience has shown that developing scorecards in isolation can lead to problems such as inclusion of characteristics that are no longer collected, legally suspect, or difficult to collect operationally, and devising of strategies that result in "surprises" or are unimplementable. The level of involvement of staff members varies, and different staff members are required at various key stages of the process. By understanding the types of resources required for a successful scorecard development and implementation project, one will also start to appreciate the business and operational considerations that go into such projects.

SCORECARD DEVELOPMENT ROLES

At a minimum, the following main participants are required:

Scorecard Developer

The Scorecard Developer is the person who performs the statistical analyses needed to develop scorecards. This person usually has:

- Subject matter expertise in performing data mining and statistical analyses
- An in-depth knowledge of the various databases in the company
- An in-depth understanding of statistical principles, in particular those related to predictive modeling
- Business experience in the implementation and usage of risk models

This person ensures that data is collected according to specifications, that all data quirks are taken into account, and that the scorecard development process is statistically valid.

Product or Portfolio Risk Manager/Credit Scoring Manager

The Risk Manager is responsible for the management of the company's portfolio and usage of scorecards. This person usually has:

- Subject matter expertise in the development and implementation of risk strategies using scores
- An in-depth understanding of corporate risk policies and procedures
- An in-depth understanding of the risk profile of the company's customers and applicants for products/services
- A good understanding of the various implementation platforms for risk scoring and strategy implementation in the company
- Knowledge of legal issues surrounding usage of particular characteristics/processes to adjudicate credit applications
- Knowledge of credit application processing and customer management processes in the company

This person ensures that business considerations are given sufficient thought in the design and implementation of scorecards. He or she would also contribute heavily to the development of strategies and to gauging possible impacts of those strategies on customers and the various areas of the organization. Risk Managers may also be able to use some of their experience to point Scorecard Developers in a particular direction, or to give special consideration to certain data elements. Experienced Risk Managers are also aware of historical changes in the market, and will be able to adjust expected performance numbers if required. Scorecards are developed to help in decision making—and anticipating change is key.

Product Manager(s)

The Product Manager is responsible for the management of the company's product(s), and usually has:

- Subject matter expertise in the development and implementation of product-marketing strategies
- An in-depth knowledge of the company's typical client base and target markets
- Knowledge of future product development and marketing direction

Product Managers can offer key insights into the client base, and assist during segmentation selection, selection of characteristics, and gauging impact of strategies. They also coordinate design of new application forms where new information is to be collected. Segmentation offers the opportunity to assess risk for increasingly specific populations—the involvement of marketing in this effort can ensure that scorecard segmentation is in line with the organization's intended target markets. This approach produces the best results for the most valued segments and harmonizes marketing and risk directions.

Operational Manager(s)

The Operational Manager is responsible for the management of departments such as Collections, Application Processing, Adjudication (when separate from Risk Management), and Claims. Any strategy developed using scorecards, such as changes to cutoff levels, will impact these departments. Operational Managers have direct contact with customers, and usually have:

- Subject matter expertise in the implementation and execution of corporate strategies and procedures
- An in-depth knowledge of customer-related issues

Operational Managers can alert the Scorecard Developers on issues such as difficulties in data collection and interpretation by front-line staff, impact on the portfolio of various strategies, and other issues relating to the implementation of scorecards and strategies. Staff from Adjudication, Collections, and Fraud departments can also offer experience-based insight into factors that are predictive of negative behavior, which helps greatly when selecting characteristics for analysis. A best practice for delinquency scorecard development is to interview adjudication/collections staff during the project to get their input. A good question to ask is, "What characteristics do you see in bad accounts, and have they changed over the last few years?" The objective here is to tap experience, and discover insights that may not be obvious from analyzing data alone. Application scorecards are usually developed on data that may be two years old, and collections staff may be able to identify any trends or changes that need to be incorporated into analyses. This exercise also provides an opportunity to test and validate experience within the organization. The same can be done with adjudication staff (credit analysts). This would be especially helpful for those developing scorecards for the first time. These interviews will enable them to tap into existing experience to identify generally predictive characteristics.

Project Manager

The Project Manager is responsible for the overall management of the project, including creation of the project plan and timelines, integration of the development and implementation processes, and management of other project resources. The Project Manager usually has:

- Subject matter expertise in the management of projects
- An in-depth understanding of the relevant corporate areas involved in the project

IT/IS Managers

IT Managers are responsible for the management of the various software and hardware products used in the company. They sometimes have added responsibilities for corporate data warehouses. They usually have:

- Subject matter expertise in the software and hardware products involved in risk management and risk scoring implementation
- In-depth knowledge of corporate data and procedures to introduce changes to data processing
- Knowledge of processing data from external data providers

IT Managers can alert Scorecard Developers to issues related to data collection and coding—particularly when new data is introduced—and to implementation issues related to the software platforms being used to implement scorecards and manipulate data. They must be notified of changes to maintain timelines for implementation. In particular, where scorecards are being developed using complex transformations or calculations, and they need to be implemented on real-time software, the IT department may be able to advise if these calculations are beyond the capabilities of the software. The same is true for derived bureau variables where the derivations have to be done on credit bureau interfaces or using other software.

Enterprise Risk/Corporate Risk Management Staff (Where Applicable)

Enterprise risk departments are responsible for the management of both financial and operational risks at a corporate level (as opposed to the product level). They are usually also involved in capital allocation, oversight of the risk function, and hedging. They usually have:

- Subject matter expertise on corporate policies on risk management and risk tolerance levels
- In-depth knowledge of impacts on capital allocation/hedging, and so forth, of introductions to changes in risk adjudication
- In-depth knowledge of actuarial practices

Enterprise risk staff is usually advised when new strategies change the risk profile of the company's portfolio. Increasing or decreasing risk levels affect the amount of capital a company needs to allocate. Taking significant additional risks may also be in contravention of the company's stated risk profile target, and may potentially affect its own credit rating. Enterprise risk staff will ensure that all strategies comply with corporate risk guidelines, and that the company is sufficiently capitalized for its risk profile.

Legal Staff

Credit granting in most jurisdictions is subject to laws and regulations that determine methods that can be used to assess creditworthiness, and characteristics that cannot be used in this effort. A good practice is to submit a list of proposed segmentation and scorecard characteristics to the Legal department, to ensure that none of them is in contravention of existing laws and regulations.

INTELLIGENT SCORECARD DEVELOPMENT

Involving these resources in the scorecard development and implementation project helps to incorporate collective organizational knowledge and experience and produces scorecards that are more likely to fulfill business requirements. Most of this corporate intelligence is not documented; therefore, the only effective way to introduce it into credit scoring is to involve the relevant resources in the development and implementation process itself. This is the basis for intelligent scorecard development.

NOTE:

Bearing in mind that different companies may have differing titles for similar functions, the preceding material is meant to reflect the typical parties needed to ensure that a developed scorecard is well balanced, with considerations from different stakeholders in a company. Actual participants may vary.

SCORECARD DEVELOPMENT AND IMPLEMENTATION PROCESS: OVERVIEW

When the appropriate participants have been selected to develop a scorecard, it is helpful to review the main stages of the scorecard development and implementation process, and to be sure that you understand the tasks associated with each stage. The following list describes the stages and tasks. Detailed descriptions of each stage are in the chapters that follow.

STAGE 1. PRELIMINARIES AND PLANNING

- Create business plan
- Identify organizational objectives and scorecard role
- Determine internal versus external development and scorecard type
- Create project plan
- Identify project risks
- Identify project team and responsibilities

STAGE 2. DATA REVIEW AND PROJECT PARAMETERS

- Data availability and quality
- Data gathering for definition of project parameters
- Definition of project parameters

- Performance window and sample window
- Performance categories definition (target)
- Exclusions
- Segmentation
- Methodology
- Review of implementation plan

STAGE 3. DEVELOPMENT DATABASE CREATION

- Development sample specifications
- Sampling
- Development data collection and construction
- Adjustment for prior probabilities (factoring)

STAGE 4. SCORECARD DEVELOPMENT

- Exploring data
- Identifying missing values and outliers
- Correlation
- Initial characteristic analysis
- Preliminary scorecard
- Reject inference
- Final scorecard production
- Scorecard scaling
- Choosing a scorecard
- Validation

STAGE 5. SCORECARD MANAGEMENT REPORTS

- Gains tables
- Characteristic reports

STAGE 6. SCORECARD IMPLEMENTATION

- Preimplementation validation
- Strategy development
  - Scoring strategy
  - Setting cutoffs
  - Policy rules
  - Overrides

STAGE 7. POSTIMPLEMENTATION

- Scorecard and portfolio monitoring reports
  - Scorecard management reports
  - Portfolio performance reports

CHAPTER 3

Scorecard Development Process, Stage 1: Preliminaries and Planning

Scorecard development projects do not start with the acquisition of data. Intelligent scorecard development requires proper planning before any analytical work can start. This includes identifying the reason or objective for the project, identifying the key participants in the development and implementation of the scorecards, and assigning tasks to these individuals so that everyone is aware of what is required from them.

CREATE BUSINESS PLAN

Identify Organizational Objectives and Scorecard Role

The first step in any scorecard development project is the identification and prioritization of organizational objectives for that project. This provides a focus point and helps in prioritizing competing issues (e.g., increasing revenue vs. decreasing losses) that come up during development. It also ensures a viable and smooth project, one with no "surprises"—for example, deciding whether to set the application approval score cutoff lower to get more accounts or to set it higher to reduce losses.

Examples of organizational objectives include:

- Reduction in bad debt/bankruptcy/claims/fraud
- Increase in approval rates or market share in areas such as secured loans, where low delinquency presents expansion opportunities
- Increased profitability
- Increased operational efficiency (e.g., to better manage workflow in an adjudication environment)
- Cost savings or faster turnaround through automation of adjudication using scorecards
- Better predictive power (compared to existing custom or bureau scorecard)

Organizational objectives will also impact how postdevelopment validation is done and will determine the selection of "best" scorecard where more than one has been developed. Typically, most organizations will have a mixture of objectives, including those from the preceding list.

An additional issue that should be clarified at this stage is the extent of the scorecard's role in the adjudication process—is it a sole arbiter, or will it be used as a decision support tool? This is particularly important for organizations that have not previously used risk scoring, since the introduction of scorecards will likely have an impact on organizational culture and operations. Scorecards can be used in the decision-making process to differing extents, depending on product applied for, organizational culture and structure, and legal and compliance issues. For example, a credit card company may use risk scorecards as the primary adjudication tool, a sole arbiter, with a small portion—for example, 3%—of selected applicants (typically based on scores and policy rules) routed to a credit analyst for additional checks. In this case, the majority of decisions will be made automatically, and solely by the scorecard, with no human intervention beyond keying data.

On the other end of the spectrum, a mortgage company or an insurance underwriter may use risk scoring as one of several measures to gauge the creditworthiness (or claims risk) of applicants, with substantial human involvement and judgmental considerations.

Understanding these issues will help in designing effective scorecards and strategies that are appropriate for the organization. The goal here is to position scorecards as part of a coherent and consistent decision-making process within an organization. The contents of the scorecard should preferably not be duplicated elsewhere. For example, in a sole arbiter setting, the scorecard should be based on as many independent data items as possible (as opposed to a scorecard with few characteristics representing limited information types). Conceptually, the scorecard here should mimic what a good, experienced adjudicator would look for in a credit application (i.e., an overall evaluation of the person's creditworthiness). The scorecard should therefore be as complete a risk profile of an applicant as possible.

In decision support settings, the scorecard characteristics should complement the other considerations being used to evaluate credit. For example, if policy rules are being used, then the factors contained in those policy rules should preferably be kept out of the scorecard. This is to ensure consistency and efficient use of all information at hand. In addition, if overriding is taking place, understanding its extent, and some of the factors that are used to override will help in identifying any biased data.

Internal versus External Development and Scorecard Type

Where relevant, the business plan should address whether the scorecards are better developed in-house or by external vendors, and provide reasoning. Where sufficient data exists for custom scorecards, this decision can depend on factors such as resource availability, expertise in scorecard development for a particular product, time frame for internal versus external development, and cost of acquiring scorecards compared to internal development.

In cases where sufficient data does not exist or where accessibility and quality of data are questionable, generic scorecards from an external vendor or credit bureau may be needed. Further cases for generic cards occur when a company is marketing to a new segment, channel, or product for which it has no previous data, but where industry data is available; when the business volume of a product does not justify the cost of developing a custom scorecard; or when a product launch schedule does not allow for enough time to develop a custom scorecard.

In some cases, it may not be possible to use statistically developed scorecards, custom or generic. This is usually due to very low volumes, to perceived benefits that do not justify the costs associated with any scorecard development, or to a product for which no generic model is available or appropriate. In these circumstances, it may be necessary to develop a judgment-based adjudication model. Such models are also known as "expert systems" or "experience-based models."

The development of such a model involves selecting a group of characteristics judged to be good predictors of risk, and assigning points to each attribute, as with statistically developed models. The exercise, however, is done based on collective experience and intuition, and the resulting model is typically implemented in conjunction with policy rules. Although not statistically developed, the judgmental model can provide a more consistent and objective decision-making tool than adjudication by individual adjudicators.

The development of judgmental models should be done with participation from Marketing, Adjudication, Risk Management, and other pertinent departments.

CREATE PROJECT PLAN

The project plan should include a clearly defined project scope and timelines, and address issues such as deliverables and implementation strategy. The project plan should include all foreseeable contingencies and risks, and ensure that continuity between development and postdevelopment processes is present. This is to allow seamless transition from the development team to those responsible for testing, strategy development, and implementation. Proper planning at this stage will prevent scenarios such as scorecards being developed by a group but not being implemented, because the IT department was not told early enough, or because reporting for new scorecards cannot be produced in time for implementation. All the stakeholders involved should be aware of what needs to be done, by whom, and when.

Identify Project Risks

The success of scorecard development projects is dependent on various connected processes, with each ensuing process only able to start once the previous one is satisfactorily completed. As an empirically derived solution, the process is also completely reliant on development data. As a result, there are several risks associated with scorecard development projects, including:

- Nonavailability of data or insufficient data
- Poor quality of data (dirty or unreliable)
- Delays/difficulties in accessing data
- Nonpredictive or weak data
- Scorecard characteristics or derivations that cannot be handled by operational systems
- Changes in organizational direction/priorities
- Possible implementation delays
- Other legal or operational issues

Project risks, "show stoppers," and other factors that can potentially affect the quality of the scorecard should be identified at this stage and, where necessary, backup plans should be formulated.

Identify Project Team

The project plan also identifies all the stakeholders for the project and assembles a multidepartmental project team. A list of suggested team members has been provided in Chapter 2.

The list of project team members should identify roles and responsibilities, executive sponsors, and members whose signoffs are required for successful completion of various development stages. A further list should also be created for those who need to be kept informed of interim results, timelines, and proposed strategies. These are typically departments that do not have a direct role in the development itself, but that will be impacted by changes in strategy.

Following the approval of a business plan outlining the case for using scorecards, the complete project plan, scope, and deliverables are signed off by the executive sponsors and managers from departments performing the actual scorecard development and implementation.

The purpose of such business planning is not to create additional bureaucratic layers for Scorecard Developers. The concept is simple—in large organizations where disparate departments share the work involved in the development, implementation, and management of scorecards, some coordination is necessary for efficiency and for managing expectations. The scorecard delivery meeting is not a good time to find out that the scorecard you just spent two months developing cannot be implemented. Such business planning need not be formal—as long as all the issues have been given sufficient thought.

WHY "SCORECARD" FORMAT?

This book deals with the development of a traditional scorecard, as shown in Exhibit 1.1. While it is recognized that predictive models are also developed in other formats, such as SAS code and C code, the scorecard format is the most commonly used in the industry. Some of the reasons why this format is preferred are:

- This format is the easiest to interpret, and it appeals to a broad range of Risk Managers and analysts who do not have advanced knowledge of statistics or data mining.
- Reasons for declines, low scores, or high scores can be explained to customers, auditors, regulators, senior management, and other staff, in simple business terms.

- The development process for these scorecards is not a black box, and is widely understood. As such, it can easily meet any regulatory requirement on method transparency.

- The scorecard is very easy to diagnose and monitor, using standard reports. The structure of the scorecard also means that analysts can perform these functions without having in-depth knowledge of statistics or programming. This makes the scorecard an effective tool to manage risk.

CHAPTER 4

Scorecard Development Process, Stage 2: Data Review and Project Parameters

This stage is likely the longest and most labor-intensive phase of scorecard development. It is designed to determine whether scorecard development is feasible and to set high-level parameters for the project. The parameters include exclusions, target definition, sample window, and performance window.

DATA AVAILABILITY AND QUALITY

This phase first addresses the issue of data availability, in the contexts of quality and quantity. Reliable and clean data is needed for scorecard development, with a minimum acceptable number of "goods" and "bads." This process is made easier and more efficient where the data is housed within data marts or data warehouses.

The quantity of data needed varies, but in general, it should fulfill the requirements of statistical significance and randomness. At this phase, exact numbers are not critical, since that is dependent on the "bad" definition to be set in the next phase. However, as a rule of thumb, for application scorecard development there should be approximately 2,000 "bad" accounts and 2,000 "good" accounts that can be randomly selected for each proposed scorecard, from a group of approved accounts opened within a defined time frame. For behavior scorecards, these would be from a group of accounts that were current at a given point in time, or at a certain delinquency status for collections scoring. A further 2,000 declined applications may also be required for application scorecards where reject inference is to be performed. The organization's loss/delinquency/claims, or other performance reports, and volume of applications should provide an initial idea of whether this target can be met. Typically, it is more difficult to find enough "bad" accounts than "good" ones.

The project team will also need to determine whether internal data intended for scorecard development has been tampered with, or is unreliable due to other reasons. Demographic data, and other application data items that are not verified, such as income, are more susceptible to being misrepresented, but items such as credit bureau data, real estate data, financial ratios, and so forth are more robust and can be used. If it is determined, for example, that data from application forms or branches is not reliable, scorecards can still be developed solely from bureau data.

Once it is determined that there is sufficient good-quality internal data to proceed, external data needs must be evaluated, quantified, and defined. The organization may decide to develop scorecards based on internal data alone, or may choose to supplement this data from external sources such as credit bureaus, central claims repositories, geodemographic data providers, and so forth. Some organizations obtain and retain such data for each applicant in electronic databases. In cases where data is not available electronically, or is retained in paper-based format, the organization may have to either key it into databases or purchase data on a "retroactive" basis from the external provider. The time frame for "retro" data extracts is specified in line with the performance and sample window definitions to be specified.

At the end of this phase, when it is determined that both quality and quantity of internal and external data can be obtained, the initial data gathering for project parameters definition can begin.

DATA GATHERING FOR DEFINITION OF PROJECT PARAMETERS

In order to define the project parameters for the scorecard development project, data must first be gathered in a database format. Project parameters primarily include determining the definitions of "good" and "bad," establishing the performance and sample windows, and defining data exclusions for use in producing the development sample and in the development process itself.

The following data items are usually collected for applications from the previous two to five years, or from a large enough sample:

- Account/identification number
- Date opened or applied
- Arrears/claims history over the life of the account
- Accept/reject indicator
- Product/channel and other segment identifiers
- Current account status (e.g., inactive, closed, lost, stolen, fraud, etc.)

For behavior scorecard development, accounts are chosen at one point in time, and their behavior analyzed over, typically, a 6- or 12-month period.

Since one of the secondary objectives of the next phase is to understand the business, further relevant data items can be added as required. Such data includes demographics by age, geography, and existing relationship; timings of special customer acquisition initiatives; average values of different bureau-based indicators; and any other criteria that will help in constructing a comprehensive profile of your organization's client base.

DEFINITION OF PROJECT PARAMETERS

The following analyses are done not only to define project parameters, but also as a way to understand the business through data.

Exclusions

Certain types of accounts need to be excluded from the development sample. In general, accounts used for development are those that you would score during normal day-to-day credit-granting operations, and those that would constitute your intended customer. Accounts that have abnormal performance—for example, frauds—and those that are adjudicated using some non–score-dependent criteria should not be part of any development sample. These can include designated accounts such as staff, VIPs, out of country, preapproved, lost/stolen cards, deceased, underage, and voluntary cancellations within the performance window. Note that some developers include canceled accounts as "indeterminate," since these accounts were scored and approved, and therefore fall into the "score during normal day-to-day operations" category. This is a better approach from a logical perspective. If there are geographic areas or markets where the company no longer operates, data from these markets should also be excluded so that the development data represents future expected status. For example, an auto loan company used to provide financing for the purchase of recreational vehicles such as snowmobiles, watercrafts, and all-terrain vehicles (ATV). However, a year ago it decided to focus on its core personal auto financing business, and stopped financing all other assets. For scorecard development purposes, the development data for this company should only include loan applications for personal autos. All others should be excluded because they will no longer be part of the applicant population for this company in the future when the scorecard is implemented.

Another way to look at exclusions is to consider it as a sample bias issue. For example, if you wanted to develop a scorecard to be applied to the residents of large cities, you would not include those who live in rural areas in the development sample. Similarly, any account or applicant type that is not going to be scored, or that is not a normal customer, should not be included.

Performance and Sample Windows and "Bad" Definition

Scorecards are developed using the assumption that "future performance will reflect past performance." Based on this assumption, the performance of previously opened accounts is analyzed in order to predict the performance of future accounts. In order to perform this analysis, we need to gather data for accounts opened during a specific time frame, and then monitor their performance for another specific length of time to determine if they were good or bad. The data collected (the variables) along with good/bad classification (the target) constitutes the development sample from which the scorecard is developed.

In Exhibit 4.1, assume a new account is approved and granted credit at a particular time. At some point in time in the future, you need to determine if this account had been good or bad (to assign performance). "Performance Window" is the time window where the performance of accounts opened during a particular time frame (i.e., the sample window) is monitored to assign class (target). "Sample Window" refers to the time frame from which known good and bad cases will be selected for the development sample. In some cases, such as fraud and bankruptcy, the performance class is already known or predetermined. It is still useful, however, to perform the analysis described next, in order to determine the ideal performance window.

A simple way to establish performance and sample windows is to analyze payment or delinquency performance of the portfolio, and plot the development of defined "bad" cases over time. A good source of this data is the monthly or quarterly cohort or vintage analysis report produced in most Credit Risk departments.

An example of a vintage analysis, for a "bad" definition of 90 days delinquent and a nine-month performance window, is shown in Exhibit 4.2. The figures highlighted (showing current delinquency status by time on books for accounts opened at different dates) are plotted for this analysis. An average of the most recent six cohorts (the highlighted number

EXHIBIT 4.1   PERFORMANCE DEFINITION

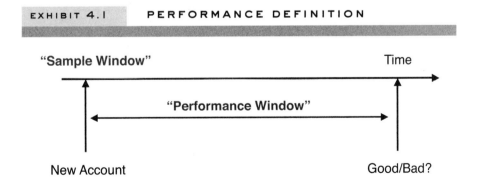

EXHIBIT 4.2 SAMPLE VINTAGE/COHORT ANALYSIS

Bad = 90 days	Time on Books								
Open Date	1 Mth	2 Mth	3 Mth	4 Mth	5 Mth	6 Mth	7 Mth	8 Mth	9 Mth
Jan-03	0.00%	0.44%	0.87%	1.40%	2.40%	2.80%	3.20%	3.60%	**4.10%**
Feb-03	0.00%	0.37%	0.88%	1.70%	2.30%	2.70%	3.30%	**3.50%**	
Mar-03	0.00%	0.42%	0.92%	1.86%	2.80%	3.00%	**3.60%**		
Apr-03	0.00%	0.65%	1.20%	1.90%	2.85%	**3.05%**			
May-03	0.00%	0.10%	0.80%	1.20%	**2.20%**				
Jun-03	0.00%	0.14%	0.79%	**1.50%**					
Jul-03	0.00%	0.23%	**0.88%**						
Aug-03	0.00%	**0.16%**							
Sep-03	**0.00%**								

and the five numbers above it) may also be used to smooth out variances. The figures refer to the proportion of accounts delinquent after certain months as customers. For example, in the first line, 2.4% of accounts opened in January 2003 were 90 days past due after five months as customers.

Exhibit 4.3 is a plot of bad rate by month opened (tenure) for a 14-month period.

EXHIBIT 4.3 BAD RATE DEVELOPMENT

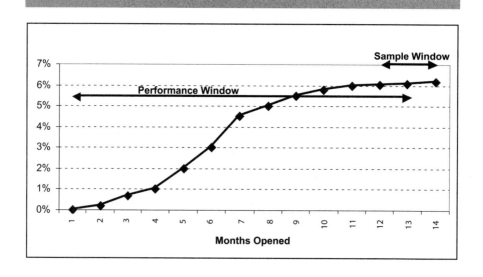

This exhibit shows an example from a typical credit card portfolio where the bad rate has been plotted for accounts opened in a 14-month period. It shows the bad rate developing rapidly in the first few months and then stabilizing as the account age nears 12 months.

The development sample is then chosen from a time period where the bad rate is deemed to be stable, or where the cohort is deemed to have matured (i.e., where the bad rate starts to level off). In the preceding example, a good sample window would be anywhere between 12 and 14 months in the past (e.g., January through March 2003), which would have a 13-month average performance window.

Selecting development samples from a mature cohort is done to minimize the chances of misclassifying performance (i.e., all accounts have been given enough time to go bad), and to ensure that the "bad" definition resulting from an immature sample will not understate the final expected bad rates. For example, if the development sample were chosen from accounts opened seven months ago, about 4.5% of the sample would be classified as bad. A mature sample for this portfolio should have a bad rate of about 6%. Therefore some accounts from this period that are bad would be erroneously labeled as good if the development sample were to be taken from that period.

The time taken for accounts to mature varies by product and by "bad" definition selected. Credit card accounts typically mature after between 18 and 24 months, while three-to-five-year-old accounts are the norm for mortgage scorecard development. This is a somewhat self-fulfilling prophecy, since credit card portfolios are by nature of a higher risk than mortgage ones, and therefore would yield the same level of delinquency much faster. Customers in distress are also more likely to stop paying their credit card accounts than to default on their mortgage payments. Similarly, and for obvious reasons, analysis done for a "bad" definition of 30 days delinquent will show faster maturity than for a "bad" definition of 60 or 90 days. Scorecards for insurance claims, fraud, bankruptcy, and other definitions will likely have unique stabilization profiles that can be determined by performing similar analyses.

Behavior scorecards for operational use are typically built for performance windows of 6 or 12 months. Collections models are typically built for performance windows of one month, but increasingly, companies are building such scorecards for shorter windows of up to two weeks, to facilitate the development of more timely collection path treatments. When developing predictive models for specific regulatory requirements—for example, the Basel II Accord—the performance window may be dictated by the regulation.

When delinquency scorecards are being built, this analysis should be repeated for several relevant delinquency definitions. This is done because the different definitions will produce differing sample counts. Various factors such as the sample window and the good/bad definition need to be juggled in some cases to obtain a large enough sample (see next section). In cases of bankruptcy or chargeoff scorecards, only one analysis is sufficient since there is only one possible definition of "bad."

Where possible, this analysis should be done using the "ever bad" definition (i.e., the account is deemed to be "bad" if it reaches the defined delinquency status at any time during the performance window). If this is not possible, normally due to data difficulties, then a "current" definition of "bad" will suffice, where the delinquency status of accounts is taken from the most recent end-of-month performance. An example is illustrated in Exhibit 4.4, showing a 24-month delinquency history for a particular account. Month "24" is the current month and the number in each "Delq" cell refers to number of months past due.

Using an "ever bad" definition, the delinquency status of this account can be classified as three months delinquent. However, using a "current bad" definition, this account would be classified as not delinquent (i.e., zero months delinquent).

EXHIBIT 4.4   TWENTY-FOUR-MONTH DELINQUENCY HISTORY FOR AN ACCOUNT

Month	1	2	3	4	5	6	7	8	9	10	11	12
Delq	0	0	1	1	0	0	0	1	2	3	0	0
Month	13	14	15	16	17	18	19	20	21	22	23	24
Delq	0	0	1	2	0	0	0	1	0	1	0	0

Effects of Seasonality

The variation of application and approval rates across time, and the effect of any seasonality, should also be established at this point. This is to ensure that the development sample (from the sample window) does not include any data from "abnormal" periods, so that the sample used for development is in line with normal business periods, representing the typical "through the door" population. The objective here is to conform to the assumption that "the future is like the past," so that the development sample is representative of future expected applicants (i.e., the "normal" customer). In practical terms this also helps to generate accurate approval rate/bad rate predictions, and more importantly, produces scorecards that will be robust and stand the test of time. In reality, such exercises are done largely to catch extreme behavior, since establishing a standard for "normal" is difficult.

There are several ways to counter the effects of abnormal periods when the applicant population does not represent the normal "through the door" population. In all cases, the reasons for the abnormality must first be established. This is best done through analysis comparing the characteristics of the average customer with the characteristics of those from the sample window. Further reasons for profile shifts can also be gleaned from information on marketing campaigns active during the sample window, or any other factor that can affect the profile of credit applicants. For example, an organization expects credit card applicants to be mostly mature men and women, but discovers that the applicants from its desired one-month sample window are mostly young men. An analysis of marketing campaigns shows that the company was actively pursuing applications at a booth in an auto show during that month (auto shows typically attract young men as customers). Equipped with this information, the company can then expand the sample window to three or more months long, to smooth out the effects of that particular month.

Another technique to "normalize" data is to filter out the source of abnormality. In the preceding example, if the company is certain that it will not target young males in the future, and that the performance of these young males will distort their overall expected portfolio, then the company may choose to exclude young males from its development sample. The resulting development sample (and portfolio statistics) will then be in line with the normal day-to-day operations of this company.

The effects of seasonality can also be countered by taking multiple sample windows, but with each having an equal performance window. For example, three samples can be taken from each of January, February, and March 2002, with performance windows of 24 months each. Therefore the "bad" for each sample will be determined for performances as of January, February, and March 2004, respectively. This is in contrast to keeping the observation date the same for all samples (e.g., determining performance as of February 2004 for all three cohorts in the example—which will result in cohorts with differing performance windows within the same sample).

In cases where taking staggered samples or expanding the sample window is not possible, and the reasons for abnormality are known and understood to be confined to one particular month, for example, it is also possible to create a sample by excluding outlying records. This, however, requires detailed information on existing distributions of characteristics during normal business periods, and it is recommended that a sample of the excluded records be analyzed for trends before being discarded.

Definition of "Bad"

This phase categorizes account performance into three primary groups: "bad," "good," and "indeterminate." For bankruptcy, chargeoff, or fraud, the definition of "bad" is fairly straightforward. For contractual-delinquency-based definitions, however, there are many choices based on levels of delinquency. It has been mentioned that each analysis (as shown in Exhibit 4.3) for different definitions of "bad" will produce a different sample count for "bad" accounts. Using some of the factors listed next, an appropriate definition is chosen for these cases.

The definition of what constitutes a "bad" account relies on several considerations:

- The definition must be in line with organizational objectives. If the objective is to increase profitability, then the definition must be set at a delinquency point where the account becomes unprofitable. This can get complicated where accounts that are, for example, chronically paying late by a month but do not roll forward to two or three months may be profitable. For insurance applications, a dollar value on claims may be appropriate. If delinquency detection is the objective, the definition will be simpler (e.g., "ever" 60 or 90 days).

- The definition must be in line with the product or purpose for which the scorecard is being built—for example, bankruptcy, fraud, claims (claim over $1,000), and collections (less than 50% recovered within three months).

- A "tighter," more stringent definition—for example, "write-off" or "120 days delinquent"—provides a more extreme (and precise) differentiation, but in some cases may yield low sample sizes.

- A "looser" definition (e.g., 30 days delinquent) will yield a higher number of accounts for the sample, but may not be a good enough differentiator between good and bad accounts, and will thus produce a weak scorecard.

- The definition must be easily interpretable and trackable (e.g., ever 90 days delinquent, bankrupt, confirmed fraud, claim over $1,000). Definitions such as "three times 30 days delinquent or twice 60 days delinquent, or once 90 days or worse," which may be more accurate reflections, are much harder to track and may not be appropriate for all companies. Choosing a simpler definition also makes for easier management, and decision making—any bad rate numbers reported will be easily understood (e.g., 4% bad means 4% of accounts have hit 90 days delinquency during their tenure).

- Companies may also select definitions based on accounting policies on write-offs.

- In some cases, it may be beneficial to have consistent definitions of "bad" across various segments and other scorecards in use within the company. This makes for easier management and decision making, especially in environments where many scorecards are used. Coupled with consistent scaling of scores, this also reduces training and programming costs when redeveloping scorecards.

- There may be regulatory or other external requirements that govern how delinquency is defined (distinct from the organization's own operational definition). Regulatory reporting requirements for the new Basel II Capital Accord is an example of this—"bad" definitions in the future may be required to be linked to economic loss, a specific default level, or a particular level of expected loss. Based on the new Basel II Capital Accord, the definition of default is generally 90 days delinquent.

In some cases, "bad" definitions are chosen by default, due to a lack of data or history (e.g., an organization only kept records for a 12-month history), so that the only "bad" definition that showed maturity during analysis (see Exhibit 4.3) was "ever 30 day." Some organizations do not keep monthly payment data, and the only option for defining "bad" is current delinquency status (compared to "ever").

Confirming the "Bad" Definition

Once an initial "bad" definition is identified using the analysis described in previous sections, further analysis can be done to confirm it, to make sure that those identified are indeed truly bad. This is more relevant where the "bad" class assignment is not definitive (i.e., based on some level of days delinquent or amount recovered). The confirmation can be done using expert judgment, analysis, or a combination of both, depending on the resources and data available. It is important to note that the methods described can provide a comfort level for the analysis performed previously—they are not definitive measures.

Consensus Method   The judgmental or consensus method involves various stakeholders from Risk, Marketing, and Operational areas getting together and reaching a consensus on the best definition of a "bad" account, based on experience and operational considerations, as well as the analysis covered in the previous sections.

Analytical Methods   Two analytical methods to confirm "bad" definitions will be described:

1. Roll rate analysis
2. Current versus worst delinquency comparison

In addition to these two, profitability analysis can also be performed to confirm that those defined as bad are unprofitable, or produce negative net present value (NPV). While this can be done easily at monolines (e.g., retail card providers), it is not an easy task at multiproduct environments such as banks.

Roll Rate Analysis   Roll rate analysis involves comparing worst delinquency in a specified "previous x" months with that in the "next x" months, and then calculating the percentage of accounts that maintain their worst delinquency, get better, or "roll forward" into the next delinquency buckets.

For example, Exhibit 4.5 shows the delinquency status of a revolving account over a 24-month period, broken into two equivalent 12-month "previous" and "next" periods.

Based on these numbers, the worst delinquency of this account in the "previous" twelve-month period is three months past due (in month 10), and two months past due (in month 16) in the "next" twelve months. This information is gathered for all accounts, and is then graphed as shown in Exhibit 4.6.

The purpose here is to identify a "point of no return" (i.e., the level of delinquency at which most accounts become incurable). Typically, a vast majority of accounts that reach 90-day delinquency do not cure— they become worse (roll forward), thus confirming that this definition

EXHIBIT 4.5   DELINQUENCY HISTORY FOR AN ACCOUNT

"Previous" 12 Months

Month	1	2	3	4	5	6	7	8	9	10	11	12
Delq	0	0	1	1	0	0	0	1	2	3	0	0

"Next" 12 Months

Month	13	14	15	16	17	18	19	20	21	22	23	24
Delq	0	0	1	2	0	0	0	1	0	1	0	0

EXHIBIT 4.6   ROLL RATE CHART

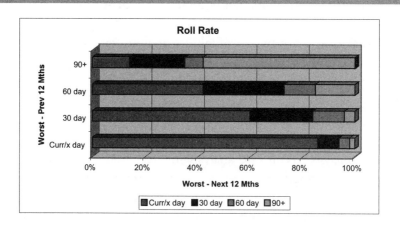

of "bad" is appropriate. In the preceding example, only about 18% of accounts that were ever 30 days delinquent in the previous 12 months rolled forward to being 60 and 90+ days delinquent, but almost 70% of accounts that reach 90-day delinquency roll forward to worse delinquency. In this case, the "ever 90 days delinquent" definition of "bad" makes more sense, as it truly isolates those that remain delinquent. Conversely, the 30-day "bad" definition will be inappropriate, since most of those accounts roll back (cure) to being current. Inconclusive evidence in this analysis may point to potential "indeterminate" status.

It is worth noting that the Basel II Capital Accord defines "default" as any point at which the bank considers the obligor unlikely to repay the debt in full, and specifies 90 days past due as a definition (individual regulators can change this to 180 for certain products).

Current versus Worst Delinquency Comparison   This method is similar in concept to the roll rate analysis, but is simpler to execute. It compares the worst (ever) delinquency status of accounts with their most current delinquency status. As with roll rate analysis, the objective here is also to look for a "point of no return." An example is shown in Exhibit 4.7.

The example shows again that out of all accounts that ever go to 30-day delinquency, a vast majority—84%—have no delinquency at present. In contrast, 60% of all accounts that go to 90-day delinquency

| EXHIBIT 4.7 | COMPARING EVER TO CURRENT DELINQUENCY |

		Worst Delinquency					
		Current	*30 days*	*60 days*	*90 days*	*120 days*	*Write-off*
Current	Current	100%	84%	53%	16%	7%	
Delinquency	30 days		12%	28%	10%	8%	
	60 days		4%	11%	14%	10%	
	90 days			8%	44%	13%	
	120 days				16%	62%	
	write-off						100%

stay at 90 days or become worse. This again confirms that a 90- or 120-day definition of "bad" is an adequate one, as long as enough cases of bads can be obtained.

It should be noted that the preceding analyses to determine and confirm "bad" definitions could be performed for both application and behavior scorecards. Even though behavior scorecards are usually developed to predict over a six-month window, it is still useful to perform this analysis to determine "bad" definitions.

"Good" and "Indeterminate"

Once the "bad" accounts are defined, the same analysis performed earlier can be used to define a "good" account. Again, this must be in line with organizational objectives and other issues discussed earlier. Defining "good" accounts is less analytical, and usually obvious. Some characteristics of a good account:

- Never delinquent or delinquent to a point where forward roll rate is less than, for example, 10%
- Profitable, or positive NPV
- No claims
- Never bankrupt
- No fraud
- Recovery rate of, e.g., 50% in collections

A point to note is that, while good accounts need to retain their status over the entire performance window, a bad account can be defined by reaching the specified delinquency stage *at any time* in the performance window (as per the "ever" definition).

Indeterminate accounts are those that do not conclusively fall into either the "good" or "bad" categories. These are accounts that do not have sufficient performance history for classification, or that have some mild delinquency with roll rates neither low enough to be classified as good, nor high enough to be bad. Indeterminates can include:

- Accounts that hit 30- or 60-day delinquency but do not roll forward (i.e., are not conclusively bad)

- Inactive and voluntarily canceled accounts, "offer declined" accounts, applications that were approved but not booked, and others that were approved but have insufficient performance history for classification

- Accounts with insufficient usage—for example, credit card accounts with a "high balance" of less than $20

- Insurance accounts with claims under a specified dollar value

- Accounts with NPV = 0

Note that some Scorecard Developers assign all canceled and "not taken up" accounts as rejects or exclude them, assuming that these were likely not their intended customers. However, accounts that cancel voluntarily are your intended customers and may have canceled due to customer service issues. If they reapplied, they would be rescored and likely approved again. Therefore, these should be included in the scorecard development process as indeterminate.

Indeterminates are only used where the "bad" definition can be established several ways, and are usually not required where the definition is clear-cut (e.g., bankrupt). As a rule of thumb, indeterminates should not exceed more than 10% to 15% of the portfolio.

Adding indeterminates to the model development dataset creates a scenario for misclassification. For example, assigning a classification of "good" to an account that has insufficient performance can result in misclassification, and the underestimation of bad rates.

In cases where the proportion of indeterminates is very high (e.g., where a large portion of inactive accounts is present), analyses should be done to address root causes of inactivity—e.g. presence of other cards with higher limits or lower interest rates, presence of other cards with better loyalty programs, or inactivity with all other cards as well. Once the reasons that credit card customers are not using the product are found, appropriate actions can be taken to remedy the situation, such as increasing limits or lowering interest rates for better customers, offering bonus loyalty points, offering product discounts for retail store cards, or canceling credit cards for those who appear inactive on all their other credit cards as well.

Only accounts defined as "good" and "bad" (and rejects for application scorecard) are used in the actual development of the scorecard. Indeterminates are added when forecasting to adequately reflect the true "through the door" population, since these are applicants who will be scored and adjudicated, and therefore all approval rate expectations must reflect their presence.

Once the "bad" definition is established, the actual portfolio "bad" rate is recorded for use in model development for cases where oversampling is done.

The discussion to this point has been limited to accounts where the performance is known. In cases such as application scorecards, where reject inference is to be used, an additional performance category needs to be included in the development sample for "declined" applications (i.e., those who were declined credit or services). This enables a development sample to be created that reflects the performance of the entire applicant population, and not just that of the approved. Reject inference is covered later in Chapter 6.

SEGMENTATION

In some cases, using several scorecards for a portfolio provides better risk differentiation than using one scorecard on everyone. This is usually the case where a population is made up of distinct subpopulations, and where one scorecard will not work efficiently for all of them (i.e., we assume that different characteristics are required to predict risk for the different subpopulations in our portfolio). The process of identifying these subpopulations is called segmentation. There are two main ways in which segmentation can be done:

1. Generating segmentation ideas based on experience and industry knowledge, and then validating these ideas using analytics
2. Generating unique segments using statistical techniques such as clustering or decision trees

In either case, any segments selected should be large enough to enable meaningful sampling for separate scorecard development. Segments that exhibit distinct risk performance, but have insufficient volume for separate scorecard development, can still be treated differently using different cutoffs or other strategy considerations.

It should also be noted that in risk scorecard development, a "distinct" population is not recognized as such based only on its defining characteristics (such as demographics), but rather on its performance. The objective is to define segments based on risk-based performance, not just risk profile.

Detecting different behavior on its own is, however, not a sufficient reason for segmentation. The difference needs to translate into measurable effects on business (e.g., lower losses, higher approval rates for that segment). An example of how to measure this is given in the "Comparing Improvement" section of this chapter.

Segmentation, whether using experience or statistical methods, should also be done with future plans in mind. Most analysis and experience is based on the past, but scorecards need to be implemented in the future, on future applicant segments. One way to achieve this is by adjusting segmentation based on, for example, the organization's intended target market. Traditionally, segmentation has been done to identify an optimum set of segments that will maximize performance—the approach suggested here is to find a set of segments for which the organization requires optimal performance, such as target markets. This approach underscores the importance of trying to maximize performance where it is most needed from a business perspective and ensures that the scorecard development process maximizes business value. This is an area where marketing staff can add value and relevance to scorecard development projects.

The Basel II Capital Accord takes a pragmatic view of segmentation by defining segments as "homogenous risk pools." This leaves individual banks across the world with the option of defining their own unique segments, without a prescriptive recipe for everyone.

Experience-Based (Heuristic) Segmentation

Experience-based segmentation includes ideas generated from business knowledge and experience, operational considerations, and industry practices. Examples of these sources include:

- Marketing/Risk Management departments detecting different applicant profiles in a specific segment
- A portfolio scored on the same scorecard with the same cutoff, but with segments displaying significantly different behavior (e.g., higher bad rates)
- New subproduct development
- Need to treat a predefined group differently (e.g., "golden group" of customers)
- Future marketing direction

Typical segmentation areas used in the industry include those based on:

- **Demographics.** Regional (province/state, internal definition, urban/rural, postal-code based, neighborhood), age, lifestyle code, time at bureau, tenure at bank
- **Product Type.** Gold/platinum cards, length of mortgage, insurance type, secured/unsecured, new versus used leases for auto, size of loan
- **Sources of Business (channel).** Store-front, take one, branch, Internet, dealers, brokers

- **Data Available.** Thin/thick (thin file denotes no trades present) and clean/dirty file (dirty denotes some negative performance) at the bureau, revolver/transactor for revolving products, SMS/voice user

- **Applicant Type.** Existing/new customer, first time home buyer/mortgage renewal, professional trade groups (e.g., engineers, doctors, etc.)

- **Product Owned.** Mortgage holders applying for credit cards at the same bank

Once ideas on segmentation are generated, further analysis needs to be done for two reasons. First, these ideas need to be confirmed with at least some empirical evidence to provide a comfort level. Second, analysis can help in better defining segments such as thin/thick file, postal code groups, and young/old age, by suggesting appropriate breakpoints (e.g., they can help answer the question "What is a thin file?" or "What is a 'young' applicant?").

One simple method to confirm segmentation ideas and to establish the need for segmentation is to analyze the risk behavior of the same characteristic across different predefined segments. If the same characteristic (e.g., "renter") predicts differently across unique segments, this may present a case for segmented scorecards. However, if the characteristic predicts risk in the same way across different segments, then additional scorecards are not required, since there is no differentiation.

Exhibit 4.8 shows observed bad rates for Residential Status and Number of Bureau Trades, segmented by age above and below 30. Observed bad rate by unsegmented attributes is also shown in the column on the far right.

In the example, there are differences in the bad rates of both renters and those living with parents, above and below 30. The same information (i.e., the attributes "Rent" and "Parents") is predicting differently for older and younger applicants. This shows that segmenting by age is a good idea. Note that if only one scorecard were used, all renters for example, would get the same points. With segmenting, renters above and below 30 will get different points, leading to better risk rankings.

EXHIBIT 4.8 BAD RATES BY ATTRIBUTES FOR
AGE-BASED SEGMENTATION

Bad Rate

	Age > 30	Age < 30	Unseg
Res Status			
Rent	2.1%	4.8%	2.9%
Own	1.3%	1.8%	1.4%
Parents	3.8%	2.0%	3.2%
Trades			
0	5.0%	2.0%	4.0%
1–3	2.0%	3.4%	2.5%
4+	1.4%	5.8%	2.3%

The same is true for applicants with "0" and "4+" trades—the same information predicts differently above and below age 30. Both these examples are based on North American data, and are explainable. People who are over 30 years of age and still live with their parents tend to be higher risks. This is also true for those who are over 30 and have no trades at the credit bureau (i.e., they hold no reported credit product). This may be more expected of younger people, but in North America, one is expected to have obtained and showed satisfactory payment behavior for several credit products by age 30, and therefore the absence of trades at this age is considered high risk.

Another way to confirm initial segmentation ideas, and to identify unique segments, is to look at observed bad rates for different selected subpopulations. This method involves analyzing the bad rates for different attributes in selected characteristics, and then identifying appropriate segments based on significantly different performance.

An example of such an analysis is given in Exhibit 4.9. This exhibit shows typical examples of three segmentations based on age, source of business, and applicant type. In the "Age" example, it can be clearly seen that the "Under 30" population is significantly worse performing than the two segments over 30. In this case, segmentations for "Over 30"/ "Under 30" will make sense. More finely defined groupings for age can also be used instead of the broadly defined groups shown in the example, if there is a need to produce more than two segments.

EXHIBIT 4.9   BAD RATES BY PREDEFINED
SEGMENTS

Attributes	Bad Rates
Age	
Over 40 yrs	1.8%
30–40 yrs	2.5%
Under 30	6.9%
Source of Business	
Internet	20%
Branch	3%
Broker	8%
Phone	14%
Applicant Type	
First-time buyer	5%
Renewal mortgage	1%

In the "Source of Business" example, all four attributes have different bad rates, and may qualify as unique segments. However, the "Internet" source may be in its infancy and a very small portion of the overall portfolio. It may make sense to combine the "Internet" and "Phone" segments in this case, and redevelop the scorecard once the Internet business has generated enough accounts to justify a separate scorecard. While this analysis is being used to illustrate segmentation, it can also be done on a quarterly basis to identify potential areas of concern for delinquency.

Both the methods described above are fairly simple to implement, and can provide some measure of comfort that the segments chosen through experience and intuition are appropriate. They can also help in selecting the right breaks—for example, for age, as shown in Exhibit 4.8—for characteristics used as a basis for segmenting.

Statistically-Based Segmentation

Clustering   Clustering is a widely used technique to identify groups that are similar to each other with respect to the input variables. Clustering, which can be used to segment databases, places objects into groups, or "clusters," suggested by the data. The objects in each cluster tend to be similar to each other in some sense, and objects in different clusters tend to be dissimilar. Two of the methods used to form clusters are K-means clustering and self-organizing maps (SOMs).

Clustering can be performed on the basis of Euclidean distances, computed from one or more quantitative variables. The observations are divided into clusters such that every observation belongs to at most one cluster.

The SOM is inspired by the way various human sensory impressions are mapped in the brain, such that spatial relations among input stimuli correspond to spatial relations among the neurons (i.e., clusters).

Exhibit 4.10 illustrates clustering based on two variables. It shows the data points forming three distinct clusters, or groups. An outlier is also visible at the bottom right-hand corner.

An example of an output for one cluster using this technique is shown in Exhibit 4.11, where the y-axis is the normalized mean.

This cluster shows the following characteristics:

- Lower than average age
- Higher than average inquiries in the last six months
- Tendency to live in Region A
- No residents in Region B

EXHIBIT 4.10   CLUSTERING

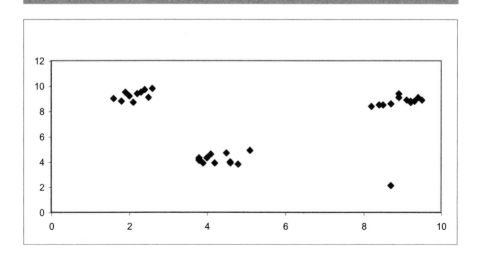

EXHIBIT 4.11   DETAILS FOR A CLUSTER

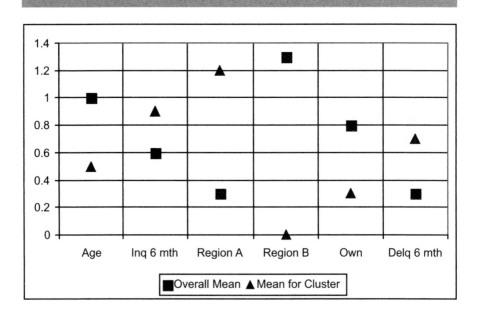

- Less likely to own their residence
- More likely to have delinquencies in the past six months

Other clusters can be analyzed for their defining characteristics using similar charts. Further analysis, including the distribution of characteristics within each cluster, may also be performed to obtain a set of rules to define each unique group. For the example in Exhibit 4.11, clusters may be defined as:

- Young homeowners in Region A
- Young renters in Region A
- Older homeowners in Region A
- Older renters in Region A

Alternatively, the clustering can be based on any of the other characteristics that provide the best differentiation between the clusters.

It should be noted that clustering identifies groups that are similar based on their characteristics—not performance. Thus, clusters may seem to be different, but may have similar risk performance. The clusters therefore should be analyzed further, using, for example, bad rate analysis, to ensure that the segmentation produced is for groups with different risk performance profiles.

Decision Trees   A further technique to perform statistical segmentation is the use of decision trees. Decision trees isolate segments based on performance criteria (i.e., differentiate between "good" and "bad"). They are also simple to understand and interpret. In addition to identifying characteristics for segmentation, decision trees also identify optimum breakpoints for each characteristic—thus representing a very powerful and convenient method for segmenting. The example in Exhibit 4.12 shows segmentation based on two levels.

The results show that there are four possible segments for this portfolio, based on existing/new customer, length of tenure, and age.

Comparing Improvement

Both experience-based and statistical analyses will yield ideas for potential segmentation, and may confirm that there are sufficient reasons for segmenting—but they do not quantify the benefits of segmenting.

EXHIBIT 4.12   SEGMENTATION USING DECISION TREES

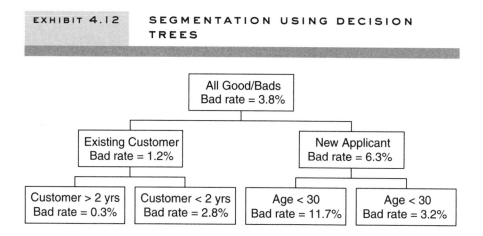

There are fairly simple ways available to estimate whether the improvement through segmentation is worth pursuing.

The first step is to measure the improvement in predictive power through segmentation. This can be done using a number of statistics such as the Kolmogorov-Smirnov (KS), c-statistic, and so on. Exhibit 4.13 shows an example of this analysis using the c-statistic (details on the c-statistic are covered later, in Chapter 6).

This exhibit shows c-statistic calculations for an unsegmented scorecard and for six scorecards segmented in various ways. "Total c-stat" refers to the c-stat for that segment based on an unsegmented scorecard. "Seg c-stat" refers to the c-stat for that segment, using a scorecard built specifically for that segment. In all cases, using segmented scorecards yields better predictive power than using an overall scorecard. Segmentation of platinum/gold cards did not yield significant improvement—probably because the credit grantor did not differentiate enough between its gold and platinum card customers historically. The best segments seem to be tenure-based, likely due to the more powerful behavior data available for use with existing clients. This analysis is based on a single-level segmentation; similar analysis can be done for more complex segmentation as well. The user then needs to decide what level of improvement is significant enough to warrant the extra development and implementation effort.

That question is best answered using business, not statistical, measures. Businesses are not run to maximize c-statistics or KS—they are run based on performance indicators such as approval rates, profits, loss

EXHIBIT 4.13   COMPARING IMPROVEMENTS THROUGH SEGMENTATION

Segment	Total c-stat	Seg c-stat	Improvement
Age < 30	0.65	0.69	6.15%
Age > 30	0.68	0.71	4.41%
Tenure < 2	0.67	0.72	7.46%
Tenure > 2	0.66	0.75	13.64%
Gold Card	0.68	0.69	1.47%
Platinum Card	0.67	0.68	1.49%
Unsegmented	0.66	—	—

rates, and so forth. It would therefore be useful to convert improved predictive power into expected portfolio performance, as shown in the example in Exhibit 4.14.

The exhibit compares two common performance measures, namely the approval rate and expected bad rate, for each segmented scorecard. It also lists the approximate size of each segment. Using a template such as this, one can decide if the combination of the size of the segment and the improvement in performance is enough to justify additional scorecard implementation. Approval and bad rates used for comparison should be based on some expected performance figure; for example, if the future desired approval rate is 70%, then the bad rate metrics should be generated for this number. In the preceding example, segmentation by tenure provides improvements in bad rates from 5.7% to 4.2%, and from 2.9% to 2.1% for those with less than two years and more than two years tenures with the bank respectively. Using these improvements, some idea of the reduction in losses in terms of dollars can be estimated.

Choosing Segments

But why would someone not implement all the scorecards built, as long as there is an improvement in predictive power or performance, regardless of size?

There are many factors to consider in implementing scorecards, including:

EXHIBIT 4.14   GAUGING BUSINESS BENEFIT OF SEGMENTATION

Segment	Size	After Segmentation		Before Segmentation	
		Approve	Bad	Approve	Bad
Total	100%	70%	3.5%	70%	4.1%
Age < 30	65%	70%	4.1%	70%	6.3%
Age > 30	35%	70%	2.7%	70%	3.6%
Tenure < 2	12%	70%	4.2%	70%	5.7%
Tenure > 2	88%	70%	2.1%	70%	2.9%
Gold Card	23%	70%	3.9%	70%	4.3%
Platinum Card	77%	70%	3.1%	70%	3.8%

- **Cost of Development.** This includes the effort involved internally and externally to produce scorecards with full documentation.
- **Cost of Implementation.** Additional scorecards cost system resources to implement, especially if nonstandard characteristics are used, or if complex code needs to be written.
- **Processing.** There are additional processing costs associated with more scorecards.
- **Strategy Development and Monitoring.** Each scorecard requires a set of associated strategies, policy rules, and monitoring reports. Creating, managing, and maintaining them require resources that may need to be hired if many scorecards are developed and used.

In cases of larger portfolios, the available resources and savings may mean that these costs and efforts are insignificant. However, in smaller portfolios and organizations, such analysis may be required to determine if the improvement in performance is significant enough to warrant the additional effort, complexity, and cost required.

METHODOLOGY

There are various mathematical techniques available to build risk prediction scorecards—for example, logistic regression, neural networks, decision trees, and so on. The most appropriate technique to be used can depend on issues such as:

- The quality of data available. A decision tree may be more appropriate for cases where there is significant missing data, or where the relationship between characteristics and targets is nonlinear.
- Type of target outcome, that is, binary (good/bad) or continuous ($ profit/loss).
- Sample sizes available.
- Implementation platforms (i.e., whether the application-processing system is able to implement a particular type of scorecard). For example, a neural network model may be ideal, but unusable, if the application-processing system is unable to implement it.

- Interpretability of results, such as the ease in which regression-developed points-based scorecards can be maintained.

- Legal compliance on methodology, usually required by local regulators to be transparent and explainable.

- Ability to track and diagnose scorecard performance.

At this point, the scaling and structure of the scorecard can also be discussed (i.e., the potential score ranges, points to double the odds, if the score itself represents the expected bad rate, etc.). The technique and intended format of the scorecard should be communicated to the Risk and IT Managers to ensure that data and theoretical issues on the identified techniques are understood—so that the results of the scorecard development exercise will be interpreted correctly, and the scorecard will be implementable when developed.

REVIEW OF IMPLEMENTATION PLAN

The additional information obtained in this phase may require changes to the original implementation plan and project timelines. In particular, if the number of scorecards needed after segmentation analysis is more than previously expected, the methodology suggested is more time-consuming or requires changes to implementation platforms, or the data requirements are expanded, the project will need more time. To ensure realistic expectations, the testing and implementation plans should be reviewed at this point. This is crucial at companies where different areas have responsibilities for development, testing, implementation, and tracking of scorecards. The Project Manager ensures that changes are understood and their impacts on the original project plan quantified, so that each phase of the project leads seamlessly into the next.

At the end of this phase, all data requirements and project plan documentation are complete, and the works related to database construction can begin.

CHAPTER 5

Scorecard Development Process, Stage 3: Development Database Creation

Following the parameters defined in Stage 2, creation of a database for scorecard development can now begin. This database will contain a set of characteristics (or predictor variables) plus a target variable for each case, which will then be used for the scorecard development itself.

DEVELOPMENT SAMPLE SPECIFICATION

Once the parameters, segmentation, and methodology for the project are established, specifications need to be produced for the creation of development sample databases to be used in the data modeling stage. Based on the results of the preceding phases, the following are specified and documented:

- Number of scorecards required and specification of each segment, including coding instructions on how to identify the various segments
- Definitions of "bad," "good," and "indeterminate"
- Portfolio bad rate and approval rates for each segment
- Performance and sample windows
- Definitions of exclusions

In addition, the following are specified and added in this stage:

- Sample size required for each segment and performance category (including "declined" for application scorecards)
- Detailed list of characteristics, from internal and external sources, required in the development sample for each segment
- Derived characteristics

Selection of Characteristics

The selection of characteristics to be included in the development sample is a critical part of the development process. This step, where characteristics are carefully selected, reinforces the need for some business thought to be put into every phase of the scorecard development project. The alternative is to import a snapshot of entire datamarts or other data repositories into the scorecard development database—which is inefficient, and unlike characteristic selection, does not increases the user's knowledge of internal data. Characteristics are preselected to make the process efficient and should be selected based on a variety of factors, including:

- **Expected Predictive Power.** This information is derived from collective experience (collections and risk analysts), previous analysis, and scorecard development projects. This is where interviewing adjudicators and collectors can help greatly.
- **Reliability and Robustness.** Some unconfirmed data may be manipulated or prone to manipulation (e.g., income), especially in cases where data input is being done by staff motivated to sell products, such as bank branches or loan brokers. In some cases it may be cost-prohibitive to confirm such data (e.g., in a low-value lending product), and such data items should therefore not be included.
- **Ease in Collection.** Data elements in application forms that are optional (and are therefore left blank by applicants) should

also be avoided, or only considered for scorecards if they are made mandatory.

- **Interpretability.** Some characteristics, such as occupation and industry type, are prone to subjective interpretation. Different people can put the same person into different occupation or industry types, and as nontraditional occupations grow, it becomes hard to slot people into traditional occupation types. This is the reason that, in most institutions, the "other" category often has as much as 75% of all cases for occupation. Even in cases where such characteristics have been shown to be predictive, concerns about future interpretation can bring their robustness into question. An exception can be made when the subjective interpretation is backed by credit risk experience. An example of this is a field such as "management quality," which can be used in scorecards for small businesses (also known as "small and medium-sized enterprises," or SMEs). While this is a subjective field, the judgment is made (or should be) by experienced adjudicators—which allows this field to be used with a higher confidence level than those mentioned previously.

- **Human Intervention.** This refers to characteristics that have been significantly influenced by human intervention (e.g., bankruptcy indicators should be avoided where bankrupts have been declined as a policy). While reject inference can remedy this situation to some extent, policy rule and scorecard characteristics should preferably be independent for coherence.

- **Legal Issues Surrounding the Usage of Certain Types of Information.** If there are characteristics that have been collected historically (e.g., marital status, gender, etc.), but are legally or politically suspect, it is better to leave them out of scorecard development.

- **Creation of Ratios Based on Business Reasoning.** Users need to avoid the "carpet bombing" approach to creating ratios that involves taking all variables in the dataset, dividing them by everything else, and then generating a list of ratios that may be predictive but are unexplainable. Any ratio created needs to be justified. For example, ratio of credit bureau inquiries in the last three months divided by inquiries in the last twelve months provides an indication of short-term credit hungriness compared to long-term credit hungriness. Similarly, short-term to long-term comparisons of other indicators such as purchases, payments, utilization, balances, payment ratios, and others, have proven to be good indicators of risk—all due to good business reasons.

- **Future Availability.** Ensure that any data item being considered for scorecard development will be collected in the future.

- **Changes in Competitive Environment.** Characteristics that may not be considered strong today may be strong predictors in the future due to industry trends such as higher credit lines or new products.

It is now known that the scorecard will be developed based on data two to three years old, and is expected to be in use for approximately the next two years. Past and expected future trends should therefore also be considered at this time. One way to do this is to consult with credit bureaus on how information has changed over the last two to three years—for example, whether indicators like balance, number of trades, utilization, credit lines, and time at bureau changed significantly over the last few years and if they are trending upwards or downwards. While this will not change development data, it can be used to manage expectations and design appropriate strategies. For example, an increase in competition will increase the average number of inquiries an applicant has at the bureau. Scorecards developed with historical data will treat those with, for example, over four inquiries in 12 months as high risk, based on historical performance. However, new data may suggest that having four inquiries is now associated with normal, medium-risk performance. Consequently, one has the option of either changing the score allocation for inquiries artificially, or adjusting the cutoff in recognition of these changes in trend. At the least, this creates an awareness of this issue that can then be addressed rather than ignored.

The breadth of issues covered in this task again underscores the need for Scorecard Developers to cooperate and consult with other members of the project team.

SAMPLING

There are two tasks that require sampling in scorecard development, namely, splitting the total sample into development and validation datasets, and deciding the proportion of goods, bads, and rejects to include in the total samples.

Development/Validation

There are various ways to split the development (sample on which the scorecard is developed) and validation ("hold") datasets. Normally, 70% to 80% of the sample is used to develop each scorecard; the remaining 20% to 30% is set aside and then used to independently test or validate the scorecard. Where sample sizes are small, the scorecard can be developed using 100% of the sample and validated using several randomly selected samples of 50% to 80% each.

Good/Bad/Reject

As mentioned earlier, typically about 2,000 each of goods, bads, and rejects are sufficient for scorecard development. This method is called oversampling and is widely used in the industry. Adjustments for oversampling (to be covered later in this chapter) are later applied to get realistic forecasts. An added benefit of using a large enough sample is that it reduces the impact of multicollinearity and makes the result of logistic regression statistically significant.[1]

Proportional sampling can also be used, as long as there are enough cases of goods and bads for statistical validity. Using proportional sampling, for example, in a portfolio with a 4% bad rate, one would need a development sample that has a 4% distribution of bads (e.g., 4,000 bads and 96,000 goods). There is no need to adjust this dataset to prior probabilities, since the sample already reflects actual probabilities.

There are also various statistical techniques available to determine optimal sample sizes based on the number of characteristics under consideration and the variability of these characteristics.

One method is to determine power curves (e.g., using PROC POWER/GLMPOWER/PSS in SAS). Alternatively, one of the two following calculations can be used:

Suppose you want to be 95% confident that the true population mean of a variable is within a specified number of units of the estimated mean you calculate from the sample—for example, you want to be 95% confident that the population mean of the average distance people drive to work is within ten miles of your estimate:

Given: z = z-statistic for the desired level of confidence (e.g., 1.96 for 95% confidence)

σ = the population standard deviation (usually unknown)

d = the (half) width of the desired interval

Then: $n = (z\sigma\, /\, d\,)^2$

In the preceding example, if you estimate σ to be 15, then $n = (1.96 *$ 15 / 10 $)^2 \approx 9$. That is, you need a sample of 9. If you estimate σ to be 30, then $n = (1.96 * 30\, /\, 10\,)^2 \approx 35$.

If you can specify the desired proportion (p) of people in your target population as more or less than the proportion you estimate from your sample, then the following gives you the appropriate sample size:

Given: z = z-statistic for the desired level of confidence (e.g., 1.96 for 95% confidence)

p = the proportion to be achieved

d = half the width of the desired confidence interval (e.g., within $d\%$ of the proportion you estimate from your sample)

Then: $n = [z^2\, p(1 - p)]\, /\, d^2$

For example, assuming the worst-case scenario (which generates the largest possible sample size) of 50/50, and a desired proportion of 5%, $n = [1.96^2 (.5 (1 - .5))]\, /\, .05^2 \approx 385$.

It must, however, be kept in mind that these are minimum sample sizes. Users should follow the sampling method they feel most comfortable with, as long as the sample sizes are sufficient to ensure satisfactory statistical and business results. Where grouped characteristic scorecards are being developed (as is detailed in this book), the end objective of any sampling method used should be that each group has a sufficient number of goods and bads to make the analysis meaningful. This includes the calculation of "weight of evidence" (WOE) for individual groups as well as establishing the WOE trend across attributes.

Development Data Collection and Construction

Based on the development sample specification, all required application (or account data for behavioral scorecards) and performance data is collated from the different sources (e.g., internal databases, credit bureau, claims repositories, real estate databases, and so forth). If some of the required data is kept in nonelectronic format, it may need to be keyed in. The end result of this exercise is a dataset that contains selected descriptive variables (characteristics) and a target variable (good/bad indicator). As with preparing for other modeling exercises, the following points are worth noting.

Random and Representative

The selection of applications and accounts must be random, representative of the segment for which the scorecard is to be developed (i.e., representative of the population that will be scored in the future), and must exclude the specified account types. A dataset skewed to a certain region or age group may not be effective for the overall applicant population, as it may penalize others or make them seem a lesser relative risk.

Nonsegmented Dataset

For projects where more than one scorecard is being developed, a separate dataset needs to be constructed for every segment, as well as one that is nonsegmented. The nonsegmented dataset is used for analysis to measure any additional "lift," or advantage, provided by segmented scorecards, such as that shown in Exhibit 4.14.

Data Quirks

When gathering this data, the user needs to be aware of historical changes to the databases, especially in the time period during and after the sample window. Most analysts who have dealt with data in financial institutions are painfully aware of situations where formats or data collection has changed—for example, the code for write-off changed from "W" to "C"; housing status was collected at field 32 until December, and is now at field 22; "other cards" is no longer collected, since last March; occupation codes grouping was changed four months ago, and so forth. Awareness of such changes ensures that the code or queries written to build the sample actually get the data as specified, and ensures "no surprises."

In most organizations, such data quirks are not documented. This leaves data miners at the mercy of their own memory, or the collective memories of those who have worked at the organization for a length of time. Clearly, such situations are neither sustainable nor efficient. Ideally, every database in the organizations should have an associated *Data Change Log*, which documents all changes to the database since inception. Changes such as those listed in the previous paragraph can then no longer be surprises, since everyone working with databases has access to known data quirks.

ADJUSTING FOR PRIOR PROBABILITIES

Oversampling is standard practice for most predictive modeling exercises (and especially when modeling rare events), and refers to cases where the proportion of good and bad cases in the development sample is different from that in the actual population. Oversampling is also known as separate, biased, choice-based, stratified, or outcome-dependent sampling.

In such cases, the development sample will need to be adjusted for prior probabilities. This method, also known as "factoring," is used to statistically adjust the development sample case counts such that the sample bad rate (and approval rate) reflects the actual population bad rate. This is useful both in the development process and when generating management reports for scorecards, such as the Gains chart. Adjusting for oversampling produces realistic forecasts and gives insights into account performance during attribute groupings—thus providing a valuable business advantage, as well as statistical benefits. Adjustments for oversampling are also necessary for generating true model validation and strength statistics such as the Kolmogorov-Smirnov, c-statistic, Gini, and so forth.

The adjustment is therefore useful when forecasts need to be produced. It is not necessary if the objective of the modeling exercise is to investigate relationships between variables and a target, or where only the rank ordering of scores is required (i.e., where a higher score is needed to denote lower risk, but not necessarily a specific bad rate). It is safe to assume that for most credit scorecard development, this adjustment will be required. Credit scoring is used to reach realistic decisions, to make very specific calculations, and to set cutoffs, and it therefore requires relationships between score and bad rates to be known.

For example, if the development sample consists of 2,000 each of goods, bads, and rejects, the sample bad rate and approval rate would be 50% and 67%. Assuming the actual approval rate is 70.5% and actual population bad rate is 12.4%, the sample factored to a 10,000 "through the door" population is shown in Exhibit 5.1.

While adjusting for oversampling can be done before or after the model is fitted, when developing grouped variable scorecards, it is beneficial to do so before the grouping exercise. This is so that the relationships between variables and the target can be assessed better—a realistic distribution of bad rate and approval rate by attribute can provide information on whether policy rules or other manual intervention has artificially affected performance (e.g., if a known negative attribute has a low approval rate, and a low bad rate, or if a known positive attribute has a high bad rate). It also provides a sanity check for any groupings done, to ensure that each group has a distinct enough performance.

There are two main methods for adjusting for oversampling: using an offset and using sampling weights.

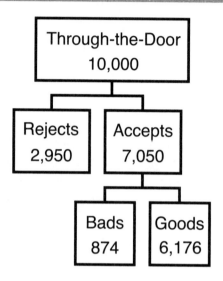

Offset Method

The standard logit function used in regression for joint sampling is:

$$\text{Logit } (p_i) = \beta_0 + \beta_1 x_1 + \ldots + \beta_k x_k$$

Where p_i, β_k, and x_k are the posterior probability, regression coefficients, and variables, respectively.

When oversampling, the logits are shifted by an *offset*, $ln\ (\rho_1 \pi_0\ /\ \rho_0 \pi_1)$, and the new logit function (the pseudomodel) becomes:

$$\text{Logit } (p^*_i) = ln\left(\frac{\rho_i\ \pi_0}{\rho_0\ \pi_1} \right) + \beta_0 + \beta_1 x_1 + \ldots + \beta_k x_k$$

Where ρ_1 and ρ_0 are proportion of target classes in the sample, and π_1 and π_0 are proportion of target classes in the population.[2]

The above is for adjustment before the model is fitted. The adjusted posterior probability can similarly be calculated after fitting the model, by using:

$$p^{\wedge}_i = \frac{(p^{\wedge}*_i \rho_0 \, \pi_1)}{[(1 - p^{\wedge}*_i) \, \rho_1 \, \pi_0 + p^{\wedge}*_i \rho_0 \, \pi_1)]}$$

Where $p^{\wedge}*_i$ is the unadjusted estimate of posterior probability.

Both of these adjustments can be done in SAS Enterprise Miner using the prior probabilities vector, or alternatively in the SAS PROC LOGISTIC step using an offset option,[3] as shown in Exhibit 5.2. Note that in both cases, the "offset calc" is $ln \, (\rho_1 \pi_0 \, / \, \rho_0 \pi_1)$.

Sampling Weights

In adjusting for oversampling using sampling weights, each case is multiplied by a set weight to make the sample reflect true population. The weights in this case are $\rho_1 \pi_1$ and $\rho_0 \pi_0$ for target classes 1 and 0, respectively.

Alternatively, the weight of each bad can be set at 1, and the weight of each good then set at $p(good)/p(bad)$, where $p(good)$ and $p(bad)$ are the probabilities of goods and bads in the actual population. For example, if

EXHIBIT 5.2	SAS CODE TO ADJUST FOR OVERSAMPLING USING THE OFFSET METHOD

Premodel adjustment	Postmodel adjustment
Data develop;	Proc logistic data=develop ...;
Set develop;	Run;
Off=(offset calc);	Proc score ... out=scored...;
Run;	Run;
Proc logistic data=develop ...;	Data scored; set scored;
Model ins=......./ **offset=off;**	**Off = (offset calc);**
Run;	**p=1 / (1+exp(-(ins-off)));**
Proc score ....;	Run;
p=1 / (1+exp(-ins));	Proc print data=scored ..;
Proc print;	Var p ......;
Var p ....;	Run;
Run;	

EXHIBIT 5.3	SAS CODE TO ADJUST FOR OVERSAMPLING USING THE WEIGHTS METHOD

```
Data develop;
Set develop;
sampwt=( π₀/ ρ₀)* (ins=0) + ( π₁/ ρ₁)* (ins=1);
Run;

Proc logistic data=develop ...;
Weight=sampwt;
Model ins=.......;

Run;
```

the bad rate—that is, p(bad)—of a portfolio is 4%, and the development sample contains 2,000 goods and 2,000 bads, the adjusted sample will show 2,000 bads and 48,000 (i.e., 0.96/0.04 * 2000) goods.

This method can be applied by using the "sampwt" option in SAS programming or a frequency variable in SAS Enterprise Miner. An example using SAS programming is shown in Exhibit 5.3.[4]

It should be noted that the resulting regression parameter estimates will be different when using the above two adjustment methods.

In general, when the linear-logistic model is correctly specified, the offset method is considered superior. When the logistic model is an approximation of some nonlinear model, then weights are better.[5] Statisticians prefer to use the offset method when developing ungrouped variable predictive models. In the case of grouped variable, points-based scorecards, however, the weight method is better, as it corrects the parameter estimates used to derive scores, instead of merely correcting the predicted probabilities. The normalization that occurs when sampling weights are used also causes less distortion in p-values and standard errors.

ENDNOTES

1. C. H. Achen. 1982. *Interpreting and Using Regression.* Beverly Hills, CA: SAGE.

2. A. J. Scott and C. J. Wild. 1986. "Fitting Logistic Regression Models under Case-Control or Choice Based Sampling." *Journal of the Royal Statistical Society* B, 48,

170–182; A. J. Scott and C. J. Wild. 1997. "Fitting Regression Models to Case-Control Data by Maximum Likelihood." *Biometrika*, 84, 57–71.

3. W. J. E. Potts and M. J. Patetta. 2001. *Predictive Modeling Using Logistic Regression: Course Notes.* Cary, NC: SAS Institute.

4. Ibid.

5. A. J. Scott and C. J. Wild. 1986. "Fitting Logistic Regression Models under Case-Control or Choice Based Sampling." 170–182.

CHAPTER 6

Scorecard Development Process, Stage 4: Scorecard Development

Once the development database is constructed, the Scorecard Developer should have a database that includes a set of characteristics and a target variable. There are various methods that can be used to develop scorecards from this data. All of them involve establishing and quantifying the relationship between the characteristics and good/bad performance (target). Scorecards or models can also be produced in different formats such as SAS code or C code.

This chapter will deal exclusively with model development using grouped attributes and a unique application of logistic regression. We will also perform reject inference, and the scorecard will have scaled points. The result will be a scorecard that looks like that shown in Exhibit 1.1. This method balances the two key requirements for successful scorecard development: need for sound statistical basis, and a realistic business focus.

Exhibit 6.1 shows the process flow that will be followed using this methodology. Note that this is for an application scorecard; behavior scorecards are developed using the same process flow, but without reject inference. For behavior scorecards, therefore, one would perform initial characteristic analysis and then move directly to final scorecard stage.

EXHIBIT 6.1 SCORECARD DEVELOPMENT STEPS

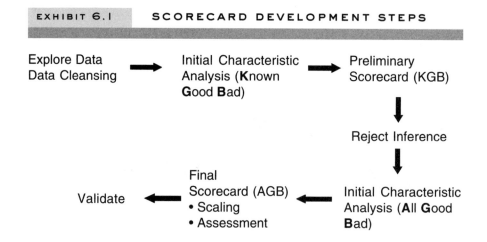

EXPLORE DATA

A good practice before actual modeling work is initiated is to explore the sample data. Simple statistics such as distributions of values, mean/median, proportion missing, and range of values for each characteristic can offer great insight into the business, and reviewing them is a good exercise for checking data integrity. Visual techniques are often excellent for this work. Sample data distributions should also be compared with overall portfolio distributions to confirm that the sample is representative of the portfolio. Data should also be checked for interpretation (e.g., to ensure that "0" represents zero and not missing values), and to confirm that any special values such as 99 or 999 are documented. This step again confirms that the data has been collected as specified, and that all aspects of the data are understood, including data quirks.

MISSING VALUES AND OUTLIERS

Most financial industry data contains missing values, or values that do not make sense for a particular characteristic. These may either be fields that were not captured, were discontinued, were not available, or were not filled out by applicants; mis-keyed values; or simply outliers denoting extreme cases.

While some statistical techniques such as decision trees are neutral to missing values, logistic regression requires complete datasets with no missing data (i.e., complete case analysis). There are four main ways to deal with missing values:

1. Exclude all data with missing values—this is complete case analysis, and in most financial industry cases, will likely result in very little data to work with.

2. Exclude characteristics or records that have significant (e.g., more than 50%) missing values from the model, especially if the level of missing is expected to continue in the future.

3. Include characteristics with missing values in the scorecard. The "missing" can then be treated as a separate attribute, grouped, and used in regression as an input. The scorecard can then be allowed to assign weights to this attribute. In some cases this assigned weight may be close to the "neutral" or mean value, but in cases where the weight is closer to another attribute, it may shed light on the exact nature of the missing values.

4. Impute missing values using statistical techniques.

While the second option may be more convenient, option 3 offers many benefits. Options 1, 2, and 4 assume that missing data holds no value—that no further information can be gleaned from analyzing the missing data. This is not necessarily true—missing values may be part of a trend, linked to other characteristics, or indicative of bad performance. Missing values are not usually random. For example, those who are new at their work may be more likely to leave the "Years at Employment" field blank on an application form. If characteristics or records with missing values are excluded, none of these insights can be made. Therefore it is recommended that missing data be included in the analysis, and be assigned points in the final scorecard. This method recognizes that missing data holds some information value, and that there is business benefit in including such data in your analysis. In addition, having assigned points for missing value in the scorecard will facilitate the scoring of applicants who leave fields blank in the applications form in the future. At the least, missing data should be analyzed first, and if it is found to be random and performance-neutral, it may be excluded or imputed.

Some data mining software, such as SAS Enterprise Miner, contains algorithms to impute missing data. Such algorithms include tree-based imputation and replacement with mean or median values. Imputation methods that consider the values of other characteristics and records are recommended for scorecard development. Assigning "most frequent" or "mean" values to missing values will cause spikes in the data, and differentiating between data with assigned mean values and data that actually had that value will not be possible—thus business information may be lost. It may be equally beneficial to assign special values to the missing (e.g., 99 or 999, or something else beyond the normal range) and include them in the analysis.

Outliers are values that fall outside of the normal range of value for a certain characteristic. For example, a distribution of age may show all the population within the range of 18 to 55, with a few at 99, 112, and 134. While these may be true, they are more likely the result of errant keying by staff. These numbers may negatively affect the regression results, and are usually excluded. In some cases, these can be assigned mean values, since they are usually small in number and will not adversely affect the results. In all cases, however, outliers should be investigated first, since they may point to problems such as fraud.

CORRELATION

The initial characteristic analysis, described in the next section, only looks at individual characteristics—no correlation, multicollinearity, or partial associations are considered at this point. However, correlation does exist and needs to be handled. Again, there are several ways to identify correlation. One such method is using PROC VARCLUS[1] in SAS. This SAS procedure uses a type of principal components analysis to identify groups of characteristics that are correlated. One can then select one or more characteristics from each group, and theoretically, represent all the information contained in the other characteristics in each of the groups. Such selection can be done based on outputs from the PROC representing the amount of information of each cluster explained by each variable and the distance of the variable from the next cluster, or a combination of the two measures. In addition, business considerations should also be used in selecting variables from this exercise, so that the final variables chosen are consistent with business reality.

PROC VARCLUS is better than using simple correlation figures, as it considers collinearity as well as correlation, and is therefore a better approach to choosing variables for scorecard development. This is consistent with the overall objective, which is the development of a scorecard, not just a correlation exercise.

Multicollinearity (MC), is not a significant concern when developing models for predictive purposes with large datasets. The effects of MC in reducing the statistical power of a model can be overcome by using a large enough sample such that the separate effects of each input can still be reliably estimated. In this case, the parameters estimates obtained through Ordinary Least Squares (OLS) regression will be reliable.[2]

Identifying correlation can be performed before or after initial characteristic analysis, but before the regression step. Both the correlation and grouping steps provide valuable information on the data at hand, and are more than just statistical exercises. While reducing the number of characteristics to be grouped (by checking for correlation first) is a time saver, one is also deprived of an opportunity to look at the nature of the relationship between many characteristics and performance. Therefore, the best approach is likely a combination of eliminating some characteristics and choosing more than one characteristic from each correlated "cluster" based on business and operational intuition. This serves to balance the need for efficiency with the opportunity to gain insights into the data.

INITIAL CHARACTERISTIC ANALYSIS

Initial characteristic analysis involves two main tasks. The first step is to assess the strength of each characteristic individually as a predictor of performance. This is also known as univariate screening, and is done to screen out weak or illogical characteristics.

The strongest characteristics are then grouped. This applies to attributes in both continuous and discrete characteristics, and is done for an obvious reason. The grouping is done because it is required to produce the scorecard format shown in Exhibit 1.1.

Scorecards can also be, and are, produced using continuous (ungrouped) characteristics. However, grouping them offers some advantages:

- It offers an easier way to deal with outliers with interval variables, and rare classes.
- Grouping makes it easy to understand relationships, and therefore gain far more knowledge of the portfolio. A chart displaying the relationship between attributes of a characteristic and performance is a much more powerful tool than a simple variable strength statistic. It allows users to explain the nature of this relationship, in addition to the strength of the relationship.
- Nonlinear dependencies can be modeled with linear models.
- It allows unprecedented control over the development process—by shaping the groups, one shapes the final composition of the scorecard.
- The process of grouping characteristics allows the user to develop insights into the behavior of risk predictors and increases knowledge of the portfolio, which can help in developing better strategies for portfolio management.

Once the strongest characteristics are grouped and ranked, variable selection is done. At the end of initial characteristic analysis, the Scorecard Developer will have a set of strong, grouped characteristics, preferably representing independent information types, for use in the regression step.

The strength of a characteristic is gauged using four main criteria:

- Predictive power of each attribute. The weight of evidence (WOE) measure is used for this purpose.
- The range and trend of weight of evidence across grouped attributes within a characteristic.

- Predictive power of the characteristic. The Information Value (IV) measure is used for this.
- Operational and business considerations (e.g., using some logic in grouping postal codes, or grouping debt service ratio to coincide with corporate policy limits).

Some analysts run other variable selection algorithms (e.g., those that rank predictive power using Chi Square or R-Square) prior to grouping characteristics. This gives them an indication of characteristic strength using independent means, and also alerts them in cases where the Information Value figure is high/low compared to other measures.

The initial characteristic analysis process can be interactive, and involvement from business users and operations staff should be encouraged. In particular, they may provide further insights into any unexpected or illogical behavior patterns and enhance the grouping of all variables.

The first step in performing this analysis is to perform initial grouping of the variables, and rank order them by IV or some other strength measure. This can be done using a number of binning techniques. In SAS Credit Scoring, the Interactive Grouping Node can be used for this.

If using other applications, a good way to start is to bin nominal variables into 50 or so equal groups, and to calculate the WOE and IV for the grouped attributes and characteristics. One can then use any spreadsheet software to fine-tune the groupings for the stronger characteristics based on principles to be outlined in the next section. Similarly for categorical characteristics, the WOE for each unique attribute and the IV of each characteristic can be calculated. One can then spend time fine-tuning the grouping for those characteristics that surpass a minimum acceptable strength. Decision trees are also often used for grouping variables. Most users, however, use them to generate initial ideas, and then use alternate software applications to interactively fine-tune the groupings.

Statistical Measures

Exhibit 6.2 shows a typical chart used in the analysis of grouped characteristics. The example shows the characteristic "age" after it has been

EXHIBIT 6.2   ANALYSIS OF GROUPED VARIABLES

Age	Count	Tot Distr	Goods	Distr Good	Bads	Distr Bad	Bad Rate	WOE
Missing	1,000	2.50%	860	2.38%	140	3.65%	14.00%	−42.719
18–22	4,000	10.00%	3,040	8.41%	960	25.00%	24.00%	−108.980
23–26	6,000	15.00%	4,920	13.61%	1,080	28.13%	18.00%	−72.613
27–29	9,000	22.50%	8,100	22.40%	900	23.44%	10.00%	−4.526
30–35	10,000	25.00%	9,500	26.27%	500	13.02%	5.00%	70.196
35–44	7,000	17.50%	6,800	18.81%	200	5.21%	2.86%	128.388
44+	3,000	7.50%	2,940	8.13%	60	1.56%	2.00%	164.934
Total	40,000	100%	36,160	100%	3,840	100%	9.60%	

Information Value = 0.668

grouped. In the exhibit, "Tot Distr," "Distr Good," and "Distr Bad" refer to the column-wise percentage distribution of the total, good, and bad cases, respectively. For example, 17.5% of all cases, 18.81% of goods, and 5.21% of bads fall in the age group 35–44.

A few things to note in Exhibit 6.2:

- "Missing" is grouped separately. The weight of this group implies that most of the missing data comes from an age group between 23 and 29.

- A general "minimum 5% in each bucket" rule has been applied to enable meaningful analysis.

- There are no groups with 0 counts for good or bad.

- The bad rate and WOE are sufficiently different from one group to the next (i.e., the grouping has been done in a way to maximize differentiation between goods and bads). This is one of the objectives of this exercise—to identify and separate attributes that differentiate well. While the absolute value of the WOE is important, the difference between the WOE of groups is key to establishing differentiation. The larger the difference between subsequent groups, the higher the predictive ability of this characteristic.

- The WOE for nonmissing values also follows a logical distribution, going from negative to positive without any reversals.

The WOE, as mentioned previously, measures the strength of each attribute, or grouped attributes, in separating good and bad accounts. It is a measure of the difference between the proportion of goods and bads in each attribute (i.e., the odds of a person with that attribute being good or bad). The WOE is based on the log of odds calculation:

$$(Distr\ Good\ /\ Distr\ Bad)$$

which measures odds of being good (e.g., for the 23–26 attribute above, this would be $13.61/28.13 = 0.48$). A person aged 23–26 has 0.48:1 odds of being good.

A more user-friendly way to calculate WOE, and one that is used in Exhibit 6.2, is:

$$\left[\ln \left(\frac{Distr\ Good}{Distr\ Bad} \right) \right] \times 100.$$

For example, the WOE of attribute 23–26 is:

$$\ln \left(\frac{0.1361}{0.2813} \right) \times 100 = -72.613.$$

Multiplication by 100 is done to make the numbers easier to work with. Negative numbers imply that the particular attribute is isolating a higher proportion of bads than goods.

Information Value, or total strength of the characteristic, comes from information theory,[3] and is measured using the formula:

$$\sum_{i=1}^{n} (Distr\ Good_i - Distr\ Bad_i) * \ln \left(\frac{Distr\ Good_i}{Distr\ Bad_i} \right)$$

Note that "Distr Good" and "Distr Bad" are used in this formula in decimal format, for example, 0.136 and 0.28.

Based on this methodology, one rule of thumb regarding IV is:

- Less than 0.02: unpredictive
- 0.02 to 0.1: weak
- 0.1 to 0.3: medium
- 0.3 +: strong

Characteristics with IV greater than 0.5 should be checked for over-predicting—they can either be kept out of the modeling process, or used in a controlled manner, such as will be described later in the "Preliminary Scorecard" section.

IV is a widely used measure in the industry, and different practitioners have different rules of thumb regarding what constitutes weak or strong characteristics.

Where the scorecard is being developed using nongrouped characteristics, statistics to evaluate predictive strength include R-square and Chi-square. Both these methods use goodness-of-fit criteria to evaluate characteristics. The R-squared technique uses a stepwise selection method that rejects characteristics that do not meet incremental R-square increase cutoffs. A typical cutoff for stepwise R-squared is 0.005. Chi-square operates in a similar fashion, with a minimum typical cutoff value of 0.5. The cutoffs can be increased if too many characteristics are retained in the model. As with the technique using grouped variables, the objective here is to select characteristics for regression (or another modeling step).

Again, it is important to note that univariate screening, whether using grouping or not, does not account for partial associations and interactions among the input characteristics. Partial association occurs when the effect of one characteristic changes in the presence of another. Multivariate methods that consider joint subsets may be preferable in this case. In any case, the purpose of doing the exercise is the same—choosing a set of strong variables for input into regression (or another technique, as appropriate).

Some modeling software offers options to group characteristics for the R-square and Chi-square methods, and to test interactions for categorical inputs. Examples of two-way interactions that can be tested are income*residential status, age*income, and so forth. This methodology goes beyond individual characteristic analysis and can produce more powerful results by considering interactions between characteristics. Interaction terms are also a way of dealing with segmentation.

A typical output from an R-square analysis is shown in Exhibit 6.3, where the incremental increase in R-square value is shown as characteristics are added to the model starting with age and ending with income.

EXHIBIT 6.3   MODEL CHARACTERISTICS

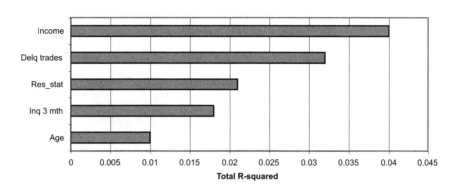

Logical Trend

The statistical strength, measured in terms of WOE and IV, is, however, not the only factor in choosing a characteristic for further analysis, or designating it as a strong predictor. In grouped scorecards, the attribute strengths must also be in a logical order, and make operational sense. For example, the distribution of attribute weight for age, from Exhibit 6.2, is plotted in Exhibit 6.4.

As can be clearly seen, apart from "missing," the other groupings in this characteristic have a linear relationship with WOE; that is, they denote a linear and logical relationship between the attributes in age and proportion of bads. This confirms business experience both in the credit and insurance sectors that younger people tend to be, in general, of a higher risk than the older population. Establishing such logical (not necessarily linear) relationships through grouping is the purpose of the initial characteristic analysis exercise. The process of arriving at a logical trend is one of trial and error, in which one balances the creation of logical trends while maintaining a sufficient IV value.

Experimenting with different groupings mostly eliminates reversals (where the trend reverses itself) and other illogical relationships. General trends can be seen by looking at the relationship between WOE and raw (ungrouped) attributes—grouping merely smoothes out

EXHIBIT 6.4   LOGICAL WOE TREND FOR AGE

Predictive Strength

the curve. In some cases, however, reversals may be reflecting actual behavior or data, and masking them can reduce the overall strength of the characteristic. These should be investigated first, to see if there is a valid business explanation for such behavior. In general, grouping serves to reduce "overfitting," whereby quirks in the data are modeled rather than the overall trend in predictiveness. Where valid nonlinear relationships occur, they should be used if an explanation using experience or industry trends can be made. Again, what needs to be confirmed is that an overall trend or profile is being modeled, and not data quirks. Business experience is the best test for this. For example, in North America, "revolving open burden" (utilization on revolving trades) has a banana-shaped curve with respect to WOE. Very low utilization accounts are higher risk, then the risk decreases up to a point, and finally risk starts increasing as utilization increases. Other valid relationships may be "U" shaped, and these should be kept as that, as long as the relationship can be explained.

Nominal variables are grouped to put attributes with similar WOE together, and, as with continuous variables, to maximize the difference from one group to the next.

Clearly, this process can be abused when it is done by someone who is not familiar with the business, which again underscores the need for it to be a collaborative process with other project team members.

Exhibit 6.5 illustrates an example of an illogical trend. In this particular dataset, this characteristic is weak and shows no logical relationship between age and good/bad performance.

Exhibit 6.6 shows two WOE relationships, both of which are logical. However, the steeper line (square markers) represents a stronger predictive relationship between age and performance. This will be reflected in its IV number.

Initial characteristic analysis involves creating business logical relationships through grouping of attributes that exceed minimum IV criteria. The alternate, purely statistical approach involves establishing relationships that only maximize IV or other measures, whether grouped or not. The business-based approach is better for several reasons, including:

- Logical relationships ensure that the final weightings after regression make sense. This also ensures that when attributes are allocated points to generate a scorecard, these points are logical

EXHIBIT 6.5   ILLOGICAL WOE TREND FOR AGE

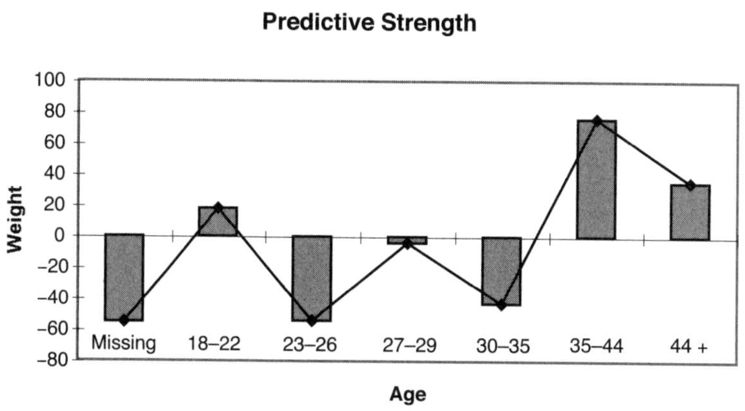

Predictive Strength

Age

EXHIBIT 6.6   LOGICAL TREND AND STRENGTH

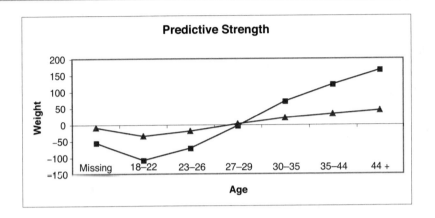

(e.g., an older person gets higher points than a younger person always).

- Logical relationships ensure buy-in from internal end users and operations departments. When the scorecard confirms general experience, it provides a higher level of confidence in automated decision making.

- Logical relationships confirm business experience, thus going one step further than a purely statistical evaluation. This allows the usage of business experience to enhance predictive modeling, and makes it relevant to business usage.

- Most important, generalizing relationships by grouping them in a logical fashion reduces overfitting. You are no longer modeling every quirk in the data by assigning an unlimited number of weights to ungrouped attributes. You are now risk ranking and modeling trends, so that the scorecard can now be applied to an incoming population with some elasticity (able to withstand some changes in the population), and that will remain stable for a longer period of time. A legitimate concern here would be that of over-generalization, whereby the model will seem to work even when the changes in the population dictate otherwise. The solution to this issue is to build a widely based risk profile, and not a scorecard with a limited number of characteristics. The long-term application differentiates credit risk scorecard development from marketing models, which are often built for specific campaigns and then discarded. Therefore, one cannot afford to model quirks.

Business/Operational Considerations

Statistical considerations and business logic have been discussed as measures used to group attributes. The third consideration is business or operational relevance.

For nonnumerical discrete—that is, nominal—values, such as postal codes or lifestyle code, the groupings are normally done based on similar weights to produce a logical trend (i.e., attributes with similar weights are grouped together). Groupings should also be investigated based on provincial, regional, urban/rural, and other operational considerations such as corporate business regions. For example, if you are building a scorecard to predict default for mortgages, grouping of postal codes should be done by similar real estate markets. It may be that the risk associated with borrowers is dependent on the real estate market, which tends to differ in large urban areas and rural areas. For example, in the United States, it may not make sense to group by New York or California as state or region, as the housing market is not uniform. Grouping New York City, Los Angeles, and San Francisco together, and rural areas in both states together, makes far more sense.

In some cases it also makes sense to have breaks concurrent with policy rules. For example, if a company policy requires loans with debt service ratios greater than 42% to be referred, then that debt service ratio should be grouped with a break at 42%. The benefits of grouping in such a way is that the distortion caused by the policy rule on the scorecard is minimized, since those affected by the policy rule are now isolated somewhat. Such groupings can also test conventional wisdom and previous policies—for example, to see if the 42% rule makes sense at that point, or if it would be better situated at a higher debt service ratio to maximize risk discrimination.

Preliminary Scorecard

Initial characteristic analysis identifies a set of strong characteristics that should be considered for the final model, and it transforms them into grouped variable format. At the preliminary scorecard stage, various predictive modeling techniques can be used to select a set of characteristics that, together, offer the most predictive power. Some of the techniques used in the industry are logistic regression, decision trees, and neural networks. In general, the final scorecards produced in this stage should consist of between 8 and 15 characteristics. This is done to ensure a stable scorecard whose predictive powers will be strong even if the profile of one or two characteristics were to change. Scorecards with too few characteristics are generally unable to withstand the test of time, as they are susceptible to minor changes in the applicant profile.

Regardless of the modeling technique used, this process should produce a scorecard consisting of the optimal combination of characteristics, taking into account issues such as:

- Correlation between characteristics
- Final statistical strength of the scorecard
- Interpretability of characteristics at the branch/adjudication department
- Implementability
- Transparency of methodology for regulatory requirements

Risk Profile Concept

Scorecards can be developed with various objectives in mind—maximizing statistical measures, efficiency (using the fewest variables), and so forth. In business terms, scorecards should be developed to mimic the thought process of a seasoned, effective adjudicator or risk analyst. A good adjudicator will never look at just four or five things from an application form or account history to make a decision. What he or she is more likely to do is look at several key measures, to form a *risk profile* of the subject. So why should scorecards or models be developed that only include four or five variables or characteristics?

The objective of the scorecard development process described in this section is to build a comprehensive risk profile of the customer. This wide-base approach not only makes the scorecard more predictive, it also makes it more stable and less susceptible to changes in one particular area. Such a risk profile should include characteristics representing as many independent types of data as possible. A credit card scorecard, for example, should include some demographic data, such as age, residential status, region, and time at employment; some credit bureau characteristics representing tenure, inquiries, trades, payment performance, financial information, and public records; some measure of capacity to service debt, such as gross debt service ratio; and, where relevant, internal performance data for existing customers.

The risk profile concept also helps in making subsequent monitoring of the scorecard more relevant. Most risk analysts would run reports such as "system stability" or "population stability" on a monthly basis to confirm the validity of the scorecard on current applicant or account populations. What these reports are effectively measuring is the change in the population *as defined by the characteristics in the scorecard* only. A broadly based risk profile scorecard would more realistically capture actual changes in the population, rather than artificially indicate change or stability, as may be the case with limited-variable scorecards.

Creating a scorecard based on a risk profile is in theory no different from other predictive modeling exercises—the difference is only in the method of arriving at the final set of characteristics. Most of the techniques mentioned in previous chapters can, and need to be, manipulated to include the issues discussed in the preceding paragraphs, since running modeling algorithms without intervention is unlikely to result in a risk profile. The remainder of this section will deal with methods used in the logistic regression technique to build such risk profile scorecards.

Logistic Regression

Logistic regression is a common technique used to develop scorecards in most financial industry applications, where the predicted variable is categorical. In cases where the predicted variable is continuous, linear regression is used. The rest of this section will deal with using multiple logistic regression to predict a binary outcome (good/bad).

Logistic regression, like most other predictive modeling methods, uses a set of predictor characteristics to predict the likelihood (or probability) of a specific outcome (the target). The equation for the logit transformation of a probability of an event is shown by:

$$\text{Logit } (p_i) = \beta_0 + \beta_1 x_1 + \ldots + \beta_k x_k$$

where
p = posterior probability of "event," given inputs
x = input variables
β_0 = intercept of the regression line
β_k = parameters

Logit transformation is log of the odds, that is, log (p(event)/p(nonevent)), and is used to linearize posterior probability and limit outcome of estimated probabilities in the model to between 0 and 1. Maximum likelihood is used to estimate parameters β_1 to β_k. These parameter estimates measure the rate of change of logit for one unit change in the input variable (adjusted for other inputs), that is, they are in fact the slopes of the regression line between the target and their respective input variables x_1 to x_k. The parameters are dependent on the unit of the input (e.g., a percentage number compared to income), and need to be standardized to ease analysis. This can be done using several methods, including using standardized estimates. Another way is to bypass the unit of input altogether, and perform the regression not against the input, but rather against the WOE of each grouping created in the previous step.

Regression needs to have a target, and a series of inputs. These inputs can have various forms. The most common way is to use the raw input data for numeric variables and create dummy variables for categorical data. Standardized estimates are then used in the analysis to neutralize the effects of input variable units. This approach is, however, not relevant when grouped variable scorecards need to be developed.

In the case of grouped variable scorecards, inputs can be in the shape of group average values for numeric variables, such as average age of each group, or some weighted average, or dummy variables for category groups. Using dummy variables for categorical variables has a serious drawback—it assumes that the difference from one categorical variable group to the next is the same. A better way to deal with grouped variables is to use the WOE of each grouping as the input. This not only solves the problems of differing input units, but also takes into account the exact trend and scale of the relationship from one group to the next. It also helps in the development of scorecards by keeping each characteristic intact. In addition, if the grouping is done right, this will also ensure that the allocation of points to each group during scorecard scaling is logical and represents the difference in the relationships between groups.

Regression can be run to find out the best possible model using all options available. This is commonly known as "all possible" regression techniques and is computationally intensive, especially if there are a lot of independent input characteristics. Far more commonly used are the three types of stepwise logistic regression techniques:

- **Forward Selection.** First selects the best one characteristic model based on the individual predictive power of each characteristic, then adds further characteristics to this model to create the best two, three, four, and so on characteristic models incrementally, until no remaining characteristics have p-values of less than some significant level (e.g., 0.5), or univariate Chi Square above a determined level. This method is efficient, but can be weak if there are too many characteristics or high correlation.

- **Backward Elimination.** The opposite of forward selection, this method starts with all the characteristics in the model and sequentially eliminates characteristics that are considered the least significant, given the other characteristics in the model, until all the remaining characteristics have a p-value below a significant level (e.g., 0.1) or based on some other measure of multivariate significance. This method allows variables of lower significance a higher chance to enter the model, much more than forward or stepwise, whereby one or two powerful variables can dominate.

- **Stepwise.** A combination of the above two techniques, this involves adding and removing characteristics dynamically from the scorecard in each step until the best combination is reached. A user can set minimum p-values (or Chi Square) required to be added to the model, or to be kept in the model.

Designing a Scorecard

While it is possible to build a scorecard by putting all the characteristics into the regression model and generating a statistically optimal outcome, this method may not produce results that are operationally ideal. The scorecard developer would typically rely on some statistical measures such as p-values, Chi Square, R-square, and others to determine the quality of the outcome. There are, however, some business goals that need to be considered when developing scorecards.

The first goal is to choose the best set of characteristics, and build the most comprehensive risk profile. The concept of creating a risk profile has been discussed earlier in the chapter. Ideally, this profile should be built using as many independent data items as possible, for example, demographics, time-related data, financial data, credit bureau inquiries, trades, payment patterns, and so on. The development process should address issues such as correlation and collinearity, and other such factors that affect the reliability of the model itself.

The scorecard developed must be coherent with the decision support structure of the organization. If the model is a sole arbiter, the need to create a comprehensive risk profile becomes even greater. If it is being used as a decision support tool, then the characteristics to be included in the scorecard must be consistent with other measures used, and not oppose them. For example, inclusion of characteristics such as bankruptcy, TDSR, previous delinquency, and so forth, that are typically included in policy rules, should be minimized.

The example in Exhibit 6.7 shows characteristics of an application delinquency scorecard that is a comprehensive risk profile. Note that it includes characteristics representing various information types, both from internal and external sources. The inclusion of the ratio of

EXHIBIT 6.7 EXAMPLE OF RISK PROFILE
SCORECARD

- Age
- Residential status
- Postal code
- Time in industry
- Time at address
- Inquiries 3 months / Inquiries 12 months
- Inquiries 12 months / Trades opened 12 months
- Trades 90 days+ as % of total
- Trades opened last 3 months / Trades opened last 12 months
- Utilization
- Number of products at bank
- Delinquency at bank
- Total debt service ratio

inquiries in the last 12 and 3 months is done to gauge short- and long-term credit hungriness. These two could also have been included independently. "Bankruptcy" and "Public Records" were not included in the scorecard, as they were used in policy rules to automatically reject applicants. "Time in industry" is used instead of "Time at employment" since time in the same industry or in continuous employment is a better indicator of risk than time at the most current job, especially in urban areas with a mobile workforce. The ratio of inquiries in the last twelve months to the number of trades opened during the same time period is a measure for the applicant's success rate in getting credit. One risk adjudicator I interviewed calls this the applicant's "batting average."

Such a scorecard is not usually a result of an autopilot regression algorithm. So how do we get a scorecard like this?

We design one.

The scorecard developer has several methods by which to influence the final shape of the model. These include forcing characteristics in, whereby characteristics deemed operationally necessary or "must have" are forced into the scorecard at the outset, and manipulating regression to maximize the chances of certain characteristics entering the final model.

One way to achieve this involves considering characteristics for entry into the model in steps, where the characteristics to be considered at each step are individually specified. This is no different from stepwise regression. An example is shown in Exhibit 6.8.

Using this technique, the regression program first selects characteristics from the same step, using either stepwise, forward, or backward logistic regression. Characteristics that pass the minimum criterion (e.g., p-value of parameter estimates based on some significance level) are added to the scorecard first (or removed first, in the case of backward regression). In the example shown, "age," "time at address," "time at bank," and "time at employment" would be regressed in the first iteration, taking into account correlation. Assume that "age" comes out as having the strongest predictive power—"age" will then be added to the model.

In the second iteration at the same level, the algorithm will consider the three remaining characteristics, taking into account the predictiveness already modeled by "age." If either one or all of the remaining characteristics add sufficient predictive power to the scorecard, they would be added. The regression would stop when no further characteristics could be added or removed from the model.

All characteristics that have entered the model in step 1 will start in the model in step 2. The regression at this step, to consider region, postal code, and province, will start with the characteristics from step 1 already in the model. Again, measures such as p-values and significance levels will be used to determine the model at this step.

Similar analyses will then be performed at each subsequent level until a final scorecard is produced. Characteristics entering the model in previous steps will be forced into the model in subsequent steps.

Statistical measures such as Chi Square or Standardized Estimates

EXHIBIT 6.8   DEFINING CHARACTERISTICS FOR EACH STEP OF REGRESSION

Step 1 Age, time at address, time at employment, time at bank
Step 2 Region, postal code, province
Step 3 Time at bureau, current customer (Y/N)
Step 4 Inquiries 3 mths, Inq 6 mths, Inq 9 mths, Inq 3 mths/12 mths
Step 5 Trades delq, trades 3 mths delq as % of total trades, current trades
Step 6 Utilization, public records
Step 7 Bankruptcy

can be used to measure the strength of the predictive model at each iteration.

An experienced user can control this process to maximize the chances of ending up with a risk profile scorecard. Relatively weaker and "preferred" characteristics can be placed in the earlier steps to maximize their chances of addition into the model, and to maximize the influence of certain variables by putting them in first and then letting the others add their respective predictive strengths.

Stronger characteristics are placed at the bottom, and may not enter the scorecard, as their predictive content may already have been modeled by one or several other criteria. Using several weaker criteria to model the behavior of one strong criterion is done for stability, without losing any predictive strength (e.g., five characteristics adding 200 points each to the scorecard are preferable to two characteristics adding 500 each). The model will be as effective, but with a broader base—corresponding to the idea of creating a risk profile.

Similar criteria are placed in the same step (e.g., age, time at work, time at home, or inquiries three months, six months, twelve months) so that correlation between the characteristics can be further considered, and the best among correlated characteristics will enter the scorecard. Related ratios should also be put in the same step as the type of information of the numerator and denominator. In addition, considering the different independent information types individually at each step maximizes the chances of at least one variable from each information type entering the final scorecard.

The regression is repeated using various combinations of characteristics at the different steps and with differing significance levels in an iterative process to get highest scorecard strength. Characteristics can be moved to higher or lower steps to produce different combinations for scorecards. These scorecards are then evaluated later using business criteria, mix of characteristics, and statistical measures of strength.

One practical way to do this is to use the model-ordering option in stepwise regression. There are two approaches that can be used:

1. Single regression
2. Multiple regression

Single Regression   One regression run is performed, and the characteristics are placed in order, based on information type and strength. Exhibit 6.9 provides an example.

Place the overall weaker information types at the top (based on average IV) and the stronger ones at the bottom. Within each information type, characteristics can be ordered from the weakest to the strongest. This ranking of each characteristic can also be done using IV. The example in Exhibit 6.9 shows characteristics ranked from weakest to strongest based on overall IV. Within each characteristic, such as Time or Inquiries, there is further ranking done based on the IV within each information type. This would be the sequence in which regression will consider each characteristic. This is a starting point, and the sequence should be adjusted in subsequent regression runs until the desired results are obtained. Another way to rank order the characteristics for a single regression is to place the characteristics in order of IV, from the lowest to the highest, regardless of information type.

EXHIBIT 6.9   INPUTS FOR SINGLE REGRESSION

	Characteristic	IV
Weaker / Weaker → Stronger	Time 1	0.02
	Time 2	0.04
	Time 3	0.06
	Demographics 1	0.09
	Demographics 2	0.12
	Demographics 3	0.2
Weaker → Stronger	Inquiries 1	0.15
	Inquiries 2	0.18
	Inquiries 3	0.19
	Inquiries 4	0.26
Stronger	Financial 1	0.25
	Financial 2	0.34

Info Type: Weaker → Stronger

Multiple Regression Using this approach, the regression step itself is repeated, considering each different information type exclusively at each step.

- Overall weaker information types are considered first in initial regression steps.
- Within each regression, characteristics are ordered from the weakest to strongest.
- Characteristics entering the scorecard in previous steps are forced into the scorecard in all following steps.

In SAS, ordered regression such as the one shown in Exhibit 6.9 can be performed in PROC LOGISTIC using the "SEQUENTIAL=" option. The "INCLUDE=" option can be used to force characteristics to remain in the scorecard, while the "START=" option starts the stepwise regression with the first x variables specified (not in any particular order) but those variables can be removed at later steps.[4]

Performing regression with specified sequences such as this can be done in SAS Enterprise Miner using the "Model Ordering" option in the regression node.[5]

Again, as with the grouping process, this approach to scorecard development is susceptible to abuse due to its flexibility. An understanding of the statistical components, as well as the data being worked with, will reduce the chances of abuse. This approach should be experimented with using several different combinations to understand data dynamics before final scorecard production.

This process combines statistical modeling (i.e., regression) with business considerations in "designing" a scorecard that is strong and stable, contains characteristics from various sources, and represents different independent information types that together form a risk profile (e.g., demographics, inquiries, previous performance, trades, etc.). Note that the regression is performed with the strongest set of characteristics chosen from the initial characteristics analysis, and that all weak criteria have been eliminated. All tests for significance are followed in selecting the final composition of the scorecard, yet that is not the only criterion for inclusion. The scorecard produced has measurable strength, and impact. Most importantly, it is a useful business tool that can be used by Risk Managers and other decision makers to create risk-adjusted strategies. Other benefits are listed in the "Risk Profile Concept" section.

Once a list of characteristics for inclusion in the scorecard is obtained, these characteristics can then be regressed again as a group, to obtain final regression parameters. Similar processes are followed for each scorecard that needs to be built, in the case of segmentations. Typically, several scorecards using different combinations of characteristics are built for each segment, and evaluated against strategic objectives to determine the final choice. A scorecard with lower "power" may deliver a stronger performance for the strategic objective (e.g., higher profit) than another with a higher power, and it is therefore a valuable exercise to compare several scorecards in this manner rather than relying solely on statistical measures. Note that scorecard selection criteria and validation will be covered in subsequent sections.

The output from this phase is several different scorecards, comprising a list of characteristics and their respective regression parameters each.

Reject Inference

All the model development analyses performed to this point were on accounts with known performance. These are commonly referred to as the "Known Good/Bad Sample." Application scorecards are developed to predict the behavior of all applicants, and using a model based on only previously approved applicants can be inaccurate ("sample bias"). This is particularly true where previous accept/decline decisions were made systematically and were not random; that is, the accepts population is a biased sample and not representative of the rejects. A method is needed to account for cases where the behavior is unknown. Note that if behavior scorecards were being developed, this phase would not be necessary.

Reject inference is a process whereby the performance of previously rejected applications is analyzed to estimate their behavior (i.e., to assign performance class). Just as there are some bads in the population that is approved, there will be some goods that have been declined. This process gives relevance to the scorecard development process by recreating the population performance for a 100% approval rate (i.e., obtaining the "population odds").

Exhibit 6.10 shows how this is created. The left side of the exhibit shows the pre-inference picture, with known goods, bads, and declined applications. In order to develop a scorecard applicable to the total applicants, the picture needs to look like the one on the right—representing the total applicants classed as good or bad.

Reasons for Reject Inference

The first reason for performing reject inference is that of relevance—ignoring rejects would produce a scorecard that is not applicable to the total applicant population. The issue of sample bias has been mentioned.

Reject inference also incorporates the influence of past decision making into the scorecard development process. This is particularly true in branch/underwriting environments, where applications are adjudicated manually by branch managers or underwriters. For example, consider a scenario where 1,000 out of 10,000 applicants for credit have some serious delinquency. Adjudicators decline 940 and accept 60 of these applicants. Subsequent performance shows that most of the 60 accepted applicants perform well and are classified as "good," which is

EXHIBIT 6.10   REJECT INFERENCE

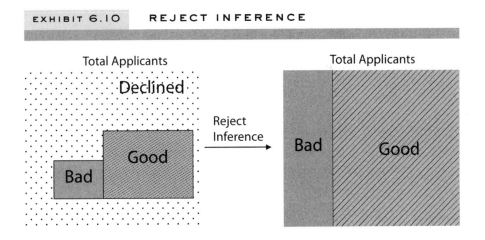

hardly surprising given that they were "cherry-picked." If a scorecard is now developed using the known goods and bads, it will tell us that those who have serious delinquency are very good credit risks. Reject inference can neutralize the distortive effects of such cherry-picking, and even policy rules, by incorporating the likelihood of cherry-picked cases being accepted into their good/bad performance.

From a decision-making perspective, reject inference enables accurate and realistic expected performance forecasts for all applicants (i.e., the people for whom the scorecard is being developed). For example, consider a bank that has traditionally approved all applicants who scored 200 points and above using their existing scorecard. The bank now feels that it has been overly conservative and wishes to approve those who score 170 to 200. If the bank has never approved these applicants in the past, how will it know the incremental level of risk it is taking by moving the cutoff lower? Reject inference, by allowing them to estimate the bad rates by score of those who were previously rejected, will help them make this decision. It also creates opportunities for better future performance through identifying the "swap set." The swap set is the exchange of known bads with inferred goods, as shown in Exhibit 6.11. Inferred goods are those who were rejected previously, but have been identified as potential goods using reject inference. These are the types of applicants that will be approved in the future. This, coupled with declining the known bads ("swap" known bads for inferred goods), will allow a credit grantor the opportunity to approve the same number of people but obtain better performance through better selection. These are business factors to enable better and more informed decision making, underlining the fact that reject inference is more than just an exercise to comply with statistical principles—it has significant business relevance.

It is also important to recognize that reject inference involves

EXHIBIT 6.11   SWAP SET

| | | Old Scorecard | |
		Approve	Decline
New	Approve	Known G	Inf G
Scorecard	Decline	Known B	Inf B

predicting an unknown, and will always carry with it a degree of uncertainty. The level of uncertainty can be reduced by using better techniques, and by judicious use. Users must understand that reject inference can lead to better decision making, but it is not, and possibly will never be, 100% accurate.

The population with both known and inferred goods and bads, known as the "All Good Bad" dataset, is used for the final scorecard production. The sample is factored again after reject inference, as shown in Exhibit 6.12. Based on our previous assumption of a 70.5% actual approval rate and a 12.4% actual population bad rate, the inference sample shows an overall bad rate of 17.9% for a 100% approval rate. Note that the bad rate for the inferred population is about 31% (914/2,950). This is a relevancy check to ensure that reject inference has been done correctly. If the inferred population has a lower bad rate than the known population, it would imply that the rejects are in fact of better quality than those approved by the company.

When Reject Inference Should Be Used   The impact and importance of reject inference in the scorecard development process are dependent on the application acceptance rate and the level of confidence in previous credit-granting criteria. A very high level of confidence, coupled

EXHIBIT 6.12   FACTORED SAMPLE AFTER REJECT INFERENCE

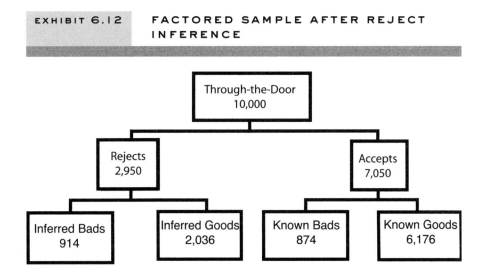

with a high approval rate (allowing the assumption of "all rejects = bad") and a very low level of confidence (assumes near random adjudication) reduce the need for reject inference. In sub-prime lending, even a medium approval rate may allow the assumption of "all rejects = bad" to be made if the level of confidence in adjudication is high.

Reject inference is also less important in environments with high approval rates and correspondingly high bad rates, since the approved population is fairly close to the total applicant population, and can be safely used as a proxy for the "through the door" population. The same is true for environments where decisions were made either randomly or using an inaccurate adjudication tool. In cases with high approval rates and very low bad rates—that is, denoting a fairly tight adjudication process—it can also be safely assumed that all rejects are bads. Reject inference will not make a significant difference here either.

In environments with both low or medium approval rates and low bad rates, reject inference helps in identifying opportunities to increase market share with risk-adjusted strategies. In this case, if the lender feels that there are enough creditworthy applicants that they are currently rejecting ("leaving money on the table"), reject inference will help them in identifying these applicants. Reject inference will also have a significant impact in cases where there is confidence in the adjudication process, but it is also believed that bad rates could be brought down through better selection.

Reject Inference Techniques

There are various techniques used in the industry to perform reject inference. A few are discussed below.

Assign All Rejects to Bads   This approach is generally not satisfactory because we know that a significant portion of the rejects would have been good, based on competitive information gathered via credit bureau files, and also random override studies conducted by issuers over the years. The only situation where this would be acceptable is one in which the approval rates are very high, for example, 97%, and there is a high degree of confidence in the adjudication process. In this case, the assumption that all rejects are bad can be made with some confidence.

Assign Rejects in the Same Proportion of Goods to Bads as Reflected in the Acceptees   For this method to be valid, one must assume that there is absolutely no consistency in the current selection system, which implies that the decisions have been made randomly up until now.

Ignore the Rejects Altogether   Build the scoring system on accepted applicants only. This implies a two-step process: (1) first select acceptees as at present, and (2) then score all accepted accounts and reject those that fall below the predetermined cutoff. This amounts to systematically second-guessing the current system, which would be ineffective, inefficient, and unpopular with those who developed, or who still have confidence in, the current credit screen.

Approve All Applications   This is the only method to find out the actual (as opposed to inferred) performance of rejected accounts. It involves approving all applications for a specific period of time (e.g., three months). This allows for collection of a sample of the true "through the door" population and their performance. Needless to say, the approved applications should be representative of all score ranges, so as not to understate or overstate the bad rate of the rejects. While this method is perhaps the most scientific and simple, the notion of approving applicants that are known to be very high-risk can be daunting (the method is also known as "buying data" for this reason). There is, however, no need to approve each and every applicant for a lengthy period of time. Consider the fact that, at minimum, about 2,000 bads are required for scorecard development. If 500 of these are to be from below cutoff, and the bad rate of accounts below cutoff is 25%, then 2,000 applicants below cutoff will need to be approved. Among options for collecting this data are:

- Approving all applicants for a specific period, enough to generate a sample of 500

- Approving all applications above cutoff, but only randomly selected ones below
- Approving all applications up to 10 or 20 points below cutoff, and randomly sampling the rest, in order to get a better sample of applications in the decision-making zone (i.e., where cutoff decisions are likely to be made)

In high-volume environments, it is also advisable that such applications be collected across a few months, to minimize seasonal variations. A further strategy to lower losses is to grant lower loans/credit lines to those below cutoff. Noteworthy is the fact that in certain jurisdictions, there may be legal hurdles to this method. Approving some and declining others with similar characteristics, or randomly approving applicants may present problems.

Similar In-House or Bureau Data Based Method   This method involves using in-house performance data for applicants declined for one product but approved for a similar product with the same lender. A related method uses performance at credit bureaus of those declined by one creditor but approved for a similar product elsewhere.

For example, a bank can get a list of applicants that were declined for a line of credit but were approved for a credit card at the same bank, or similarly, a credit card issuer can obtain a list of applicants that it declined, but who were approved by other credit card companies. The delinquency performance of these accounts at the other card company or with similar products in-house can then be monitored through their credit bureau reports or monthly performance files. The performance with other products or companies is taken as a proxy for how the declined applicants would have performed had they been originally accepted.

This method approximates actual performance, but has a few drawbacks. First, regulatory hurdles may prevent a creditor from obtaining credit bureau records of declined applicants (in some jurisdictions there is a time limit for this). This may, however, be possible if the declined applicant is an existing client of a multiproduct bank, whose credit bureau record is obtained at regular intervals by the bank. Again, in jurisdictions where the use of credit bureau records is strictly regulated, this may not be possible. The applicants chosen must also obtain *similar credit* during a *similar time frame* (i.e., soon after being declined). Further, the "bad" definition chosen through analysis of known goods and bads must be used for these accounts using different data sources—which may not be easily done. Applicants declined at one institution or for one product are also likely to be declined elsewhere, thus reducing the potential sample size.

Augmentation in Historically Judgmental Decision-Making Environment (Soft Cutoff)   This method seeks to match up people with like characteristics and count the rejects as assigned by this process. The idea behind augmentation is that people rejected at a given score will behave essentially the same as those accepted at that score. The method consists of first building an Accept/Reject scoring system, which shows the inconsistency in the current credit-granting system. Within each score interval, the number of applicants accepted and rejected is tallied. The augmentation factor is defined as: $(A + R)/A$, where A = number of acceptees in the interval, and R = number of rejects in the interval. The computer algorithm for augmentation is then:

- Setup
  - Define the number of score intervals
  - Calculate augmentation factors for all score intervals
- Loop
  - Select an acceptee sample point
  - Score the sample point in question
  - Retrieve the augmentation factor for that score interval (from Setup step 2)
  - Identify the performance group for the sample point in question
  - Tally the sample point as "n" goods or bads, depending on the performance category (from step 6)
  - Have all acceptees been examined? (No—go to step 3, Yes—the process is done)

After the augmentation factors have been applied, the number of augmented goods (AG) and augmented bads (AB) can be calculated and the population odds (AG/AB) are necessarily a convex combination of the acceptee population odds (G/B) and the reject population odds [(AG-G)/(AB-B)]. A typical ratio of the acceptee population odds to the reject population odds is 1.5 to 4.0. In a hypothetical example, suppose there are 10,000 applicants coming through the door. Suppose further that typically there are 3,500 rejects and 6,500 acceptees, composed of 300 bads and 6,200 goods. Suppose further that after augmentation there are augmented goods (AG) of 9,400 and augmented bads (AB) of 600. This implies that among the 3,500 rejects, there are 300 bads and 3,200 goods, and we may calculate the following odds ratios:

$$\text{Overall population odds: } 9,400/600 = 15.7 \text{ to } 1$$
$$\text{Acceptee population odds: } 6,200/300 = 20.7 \text{ to } 1$$
$$\text{Reject population odds: } 3,200/300 = 10.7 \text{ to } 1$$

In this hypothetical case, the acceptee population is twice the quality of the reject population. The upshot is that augmentation has allowed the scorecard developer to swap some of the accepted bads for a portion of the accepted goods.

Simple Augmentation   This method, also known as "hard cutoff," involves the following steps:

Step 1   Build a model using known goods and bads (note that this is what has been done in the previous section of this chapter).

Step 2   Score rejects using this model and establish their expected bad rates, or p(bad).

Step 3   Set an expected bad rate level above which an account is deemed "bad"; all applicants below this level are conversely classified as "good." A good and consistent selection point is at the expected marginal bad rate of the worst-quality applicant you are willing to approve today.

Step 4   Add the inferred goods and bads to the known goods/bads and remodel.

This method is simple, but has some drawbacks. The classification of rejects into goods and bads can be arbitrary, even though one can use iterations with different cutoffs and simple rules of thumb to make sanity checks (e.g., bad rate of rejected population should be two to four times that of the accepts). The known good/bad scorecard here needs to be strong since it is the only thing being used to assign class. This method also does not take into account the probability of a reject being approved, and hence rejects are incorporated into the known on a 1:1 basis. The next method seeks to remedy this particular drawback.

Augmentation 2[6]   This method adjusts the weights of the known good/bad model by an estimate of the probability of acceptance (i.e., the probability of being included in the known population). This is done in two steps:

Step 1   An accept/decline model is built to get the probability of accept or decline for each case.

Step 2   Using only the known goods and bads (i.e., the accepts), a good/bad model is built with the population distribution adjusted using the previously established accept/reject weights. This is done in such a way that the new case weights are inversely proportional to the probability of acceptance, so that cases are weighed to more accurately represent the total population.

This method recognizes the need to adjust the p(approve) and is better than simple augmentation. A similar technique that uses the rejected population is explained later under "Fuzzy Augmentation."

Parceling   This method is similar to simple augmentation, but instead of classifying all rejects at a certain score as good or bad, it assigns them in proportion to the expected bad rate at that score. Exhibit 6.13 illustrates an example:

The first four columns in the exhibit are distributions by score of the "known good/bad" sample, using the known good/bad scorecard. The "reject" column represents the distribution of rejects as scored by the

EXHIBIT 6.13   REJECT INFERENCE USING PARCELING

Score	# Bad	# Good	% Bad	% Good	Reject	Rej - Bad	Rej - Good
0–169	290	971	23.0%	77.0%	1,646	379	1,267
170–179	530	2,414	18.0%	82.0%	1,732	312	1,420
180–189	365	2,242	14.0%	86.0%	3,719	521	3,198
190–199	131	1,179	10.0%	90.0%	7,334	733	6,601
200–209	211	2,427	8.0%	92.0%	1,176	94	1,082
210–219	213	4,047	5.0%	95.0%	3,518	176	3,342
220–229	122	2,928	4.0%	96.0%	7,211	288	6,923
230–239	139	6,811	2.0%	98.0%	3,871	77	3,794
240–249	88	10,912	0.8%	99.2%	4,773	38	4,735
250+	94	18,706	0.5%	99.5%	8,982	45	8,937

known good/bad scorecard. The last two columns represent the random allocation of the scored rejects into "good" and "bad" classes.

For example, if there are 7,334 rejects in the score range 190–199, and the expected bad rate is 10.0%, 733 rejects will be assigned as "bad" and the remaining 6,601 as "good." The assignment of classes within each score band is random.

However, business sense would suggest that since the proportion of goods and bads in the rejects cannot be the same as that of the approves (rejects should be worse), a conservative approach is to assign a higher proportion of rejects as bad. An iterative approach and rules of thumb can be used here to ensure that the overall bad rate of the rejects is between two to four times that of the approved, at a minimum. A higher factor may be obtained if the previous credit granting was considered tight.

This method is also fairly quick and simple to implement. As with simple augmentation, the known good/bad scorecard here needs to be good, since it is the only thing being used to allocate class. In addition, the allocation needs to be adjusted (e.g., based on the conservative approach above) so that the bad rate of the rejects is not understated.

Fuzzy Augmentation   This method is also similar to simple augmentation, but instead of assigning a "good" or "bad" class, it assigns each reject a partial "good" and a partial "bad" class. The full process involves classification and then augmentation using the following steps:

Step1   Classification.
- Score rejects with the known good/bad model.
- Determine p(good) and p(bad) for each reject based on expected bad rates.
- Assign each reject as a partial good and a partial bad (i.e., creating two weighted cases from each reject).
- Weigh rejected goods with p(good) and rejected bads with p(bad). As with parceling, each scored reject can be assigned a higher expected p(bad) as a conservative measure.

Step 2   Augmentation.
- Combine rejects with accepts, adjusting for approval rate, p(approve).
- For example, frequency of a "good" from rejects = p(good) × weight, where "weight" is the probability of a reject being included in the augmented dataset.

The additional weighting at the augmentation step is done since combining accepts and inferred rejects on a one-to-one basis would imply that they both have equal chances of being in the dataset.

This method incorporates not just the likelihood of a reject being bad, but also its probability of being accepted in the first place. This is a better approach, as it assigns some measure of importance to a reject in the final sample. In addition, using partial classification makes it better than methods that use arbitrary measures to do so.

Iterative Reclassification[7]   This method involves first building a known good/bad model, assigning classes based on a p(bad) (as in simple augmentation), combining rejects with the accepts, and repeating the process until some convergence is reached.

The steps are as follows:

Step 1   Build a known good/bad scorecard.

Step 2   Score rejects and assign class based on a minimum expected bad rate or chosen p(bad).

Step 3   Combine the inferred rejects and accepts, and rebuild scorecard.

Step 4   Rescore the rejects and reassign class, then combine and rebuild scorecard.

Step 5   Repeat this process until parameter estimates (and p(bad)) converge.

Note that one way to modify this approach is to use partial good/bad classifications instead of classifying on the basis of an arbitrary p(bad).

Convergence can be measured by using parameter estimates or p(bad) for each score group or for each run, or by using a plot of log(odds) against score, as shown in Exhibit 6.14. The dashed lines represent iterations.

Each iteration should be below the known good/bad (KGB) line, confirming that the combined population has a higher bad rate than the accepts alone. If the combined dataset line is above the KGB line, it would imply that the rejects are of better quality than the accepts.

Nearest Neighbor (Clustering)   This technique uses clustering to identify goods and bads in a reject sample, and does not rely on any previously built models. The steps involved are fairly simple:

EXHIBIT 6.14   **REJECT INFERENCE USING ITERATIVE RECLASSIFICATION**

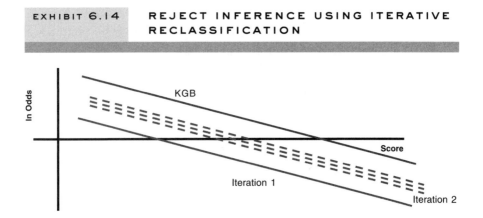

Step 1   Create two sets of clusters—one each for known goods and bads.

Step 2   Run rejects through both clusters.

Step 3   Compare Euclidean distances to assign most likely performance (i.e., if a reject is closer to a "good" cluster than a "bad" one, then it is likely a good).

Step 4   Combine accepts and rejects to create inferred dataset, and remodel.

As further steps to refine this approach, adjustment for p(approve) can be added when creating the inferred dataset, and partial classifications can be done. This method is also relatively simple to do with the right tools. Its drawback is that the measures are relative—as compared to the other options discussed in previous sections.

Memory-Based Reasoning   Memory-based, or case-based, reasoning follows a two-step process to assign class. First, it identifies similar cases, for example, good and bad cases in a sample. It then uses the learning from the first step to assign class to a new record. This process mimics the thought pattern that people would go through if they were performing manual reject inference. For example a person reviews many known good and bad accounts and notes the characteristics of both. He or she then goes through a set of rejected ones and identifies those that have similar characteristics as the known goods or bads.

The steps involved in performing reject inference using memory-based reasoning are:

Step 1   Perform clustering using the known goods, bads, and rejects. SAS Enterprise Miner, for example, uses the k-nearest neighbor algorithm to categorize observations in its Memory Based Reasoning node.

Step 2   The distance between each known good/bad observation and the reject case (called a "probe") is then measured. The k known good/bad observations that have the smallest Euclidean distance to a reject case are then the k-nearest neighbor to that reject.

Step 3 The target classes (good/bad mix) of the *k*-nearest neighbors are then used to assign a probability of good/bad to each reject case.

Step 4 Create a combined sample and remodel.

For example, if the value of *k* is set to 10, and the ten nearest neighbors to the reject are seven good and three bad cases, then the posterior probability, *p*(bad), of that reject is 30%. This can be used to make either partial classification for each reject case or full classification based on some level of *p*(bad).

Verification

Once reject inference is completed, simple analysis can be done to verify the results. This includes:

- Comparing bad rates/odds of inferred and known samples and applying industry rules of thumb as discussed previously. Reject inference can be run with different parameters until these rules of thumb are satisfied. The rules of thumb should be applied based on the approval rate and the level of confidence in previous credit granting. For example, if the previous credit granting was good, and the approval rate was also high, then the inferred rejects should have a bad rate at least three or four times that of the approves. A medium approval rate may yield an inferred bad rate only twice that of approves.

- Comparing the weight of evidence or bad rates of grouped attributes for pre- and postinferred datasets. Attributes with low acceptance rates and high WOE should display changes in their weight of evidence consistent with business experience—or in a manner explainable otherwise.

Different reject inference techniques and parameters can also be tested using "fake" rejects. This involves splitting the approved population into arbitrary accepts and rejects, for example a 70/30 split. A model developed on the 70% "approved" sample can then be used for inferring the performance of the remaining 30%. Since the actual performance of the 30% "rejects" is already known, misclassification can be used to gauge the performance of each reject inference method.

Once reject inference is completed, the combined dataset (of approves and inferred rejects) is created and used for the next phase of scorecard development. Now that sample bias is resolved, this final scorecard is applicable to the entire "through the door" population.

FINAL SCORECARD PRODUCTION

The final scorecards are then produced by running the same initial characteristic analysis and statistical algorithms (e.g., regression) on the postinferred dataset, to generate the final set of characteristics for the scorecard. Note that you are not limited to the characteristics selected in the preliminary scorecard in this phase. Some characteristics may appear weaker and some stronger after reject inference, so the process of selecting characteristics needs to be repeated, considering the entire development dataset.

At this point, let's assume that a final scorecard has been produced by performing initial characteristic analysis and logistic regression to the "All Good Bad" dataset. What we have now is a set of characteristics, along with the output from logistic regression such as the intercept, parameter estimates, and model performance statistics.

Additional issues that now need to be addressed are scaling of the scores, validity of the points allocation, misclassification, and scorecard strength.

Scaling

Scorecards can be produced in many formats (e.g., SAS and C code, points system, etc.). In some cases—such as online or real-time scorecard usage that is often dependent on implementation platforms, regulatory instructions requiring the provision of reasons for decline, ease of use, and other factors mentioned in the "Why 'Scorecard' Format" section in Chapter 3—the scorecard needs to be produced in a particular format (see Exhibit 1.1). In this case, scaling needs to be applied. Scaling refers to the range and format of scores in a scorecard and the rate of change in odds for increases in score. Scorecard scores can take several forms with decimal or discrete number scores:

- Where the score is the good/bad odd or probability of bad (e.g., score of 6 means a 6:1 odd or 6% chance of default)

- With some defined numerical minimum/maximum scale (e.g. −1, 0–1000, 150–350) with a specified odds ratio at a certain point (e.g., odds of 5:1 at 500) and specified rate of change of odds (e.g., double every 50 points)

The choice of scaling does not affect the predictive strength of the scorecard. It is an operational decision based on considerations such as:

- Implementability of the scorecard into application processing software. Certain software can only implement scorecards in the format shown in Exhibit 1.1.

- Ease of understanding by staff (e.g., discrete numbers are easier to work with).

- Continuity with existing scorecards or other scorecards in the company. This avoids retraining on scorecard usage and interpretation of scores.

There are various scales in use in the industry. One of the most common is a scorecard with discrete scores scaled logarithmically, with the odds doubling at every 20 points. An example of such scaling is shown in Exhibit 6.15.

Scaling Calculation   In general, the relationship between odds and scores can be presented as a linear transformation:

$$\text{Score} = \text{Offset} + \text{Factor } ln \text{ (odds)}$$

EXHIBIT 6.15   SCALED SCORES

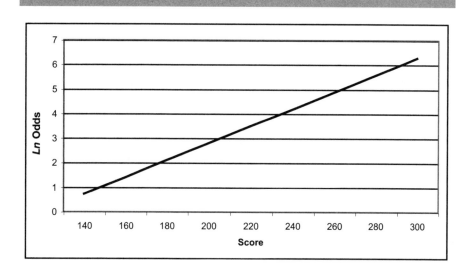

Where the scorecard is being developed using specified odds at a score and specified "points to double the odds" (*pdo*), the factor and offset can easily be calculated by using the following simultaneous equations:

$$\text{Score} = \text{Offset} + \text{Factor} * ln \, (\text{odds})$$
$$\text{Score} + pdo = \text{Offset} + \text{Factor} * ln \, (2 * \text{odds})$$

Solving the equations above for *pdo*, we get

$$pdo = \text{Factor} * ln \, (2), \text{ therefore}$$

$$\text{Factor} = pdo \, / \, ln \, (2);$$
$$\text{Offset} = \text{Score} - \{\text{Factor} * ln \, (\text{Odds})\}$$

For example, if a scorecard were being scaled where the user wanted odds of 50:1 at 600 points and wanted the odds to double every 20 points (i.e., *pdo* = 20), the factor and offset would be:

$$\text{Factor} = 20 \, / \, ln \, (2) = 28.8539$$
$$\text{Offset} = 600 - \{28.8539 \, ln \, (50)\} = 487.123$$

And each score corresponding to each set of odds (or each attribute) can be calculated as:

$$\text{Score} = 487.123 + 28.8539 \; ln \; (\text{odds})$$

The same formula can be used to scale scorecards that triple or quadruple the odds every few points. "Points to double the odds," however, is the most widely used scaling in the credit risk industry.

This formula can be used to generate scores for any case, using any model that can generate a probability of bad, or odds. This would include models developed using techniques other than regression, as has been discussed in this book.

Since the scorecard here is being developed using the weight of evidence as input, the preceding relationship can be modified as:

$$\text{score} = ln(\text{odds} * \text{factor} + \text{offset} =$$

$$-\left(\sum_{j, \, i=1}^{k, \, n} (\text{woe}_j * \beta_i) + a \right) * \text{factor} + \text{offset} =$$

$$-\left(\sum_{j, \, i=1}^{k, \, n} \left(\text{woe}_j * \beta_i + \frac{a}{n}\right) \right) * \text{factor} + \text{offset} =$$

$$\sum_{j, \, i=1}^{k, \, n} \left(-\left(\text{woe}_j * \beta_i + \frac{a}{n}\right) * \text{factor} + \frac{\text{offset}}{n} \right)$$

where
WOE = weight of evidence for each grouped attribute
β = regression coefficient for each characteristic
a = intercept term from logistic regression
n = number of characteristics
k = number of groups (of attributes) in each characteristic

The formula would calculate the scores to be assigned to each grouped attribute, for every characteristic in the scorecard developed, and summing all the scores for each attribute would then provide the final score. At this point it is worth noting that the trend and difference between weights of evidence in the grouped attributes will affect the points assigned using this approach. This underscores the emphasis placed on both maintaining a logical trend of WOE and trying to maximize the differences in the WOE of successive groups.

Adverse Codes   In some jurisdictions, notably the United States, lenders are required to give borrowers reasons for declining their applications. This is done using adverse codes. Using the methodology for allocating scores above, adverse codes can be generated by first obtaining a "neutral score." The neutral score would be the score where the WOE is 0. In the equation above, once the factor and offset are obtained, one can substitute WOE = 0 in the equation to get the neutral score. The equation for neutral score is therefore:

$$ -\left(\frac{a}{n}\right) * \text{factor} + \frac{\text{offset}}{n} $$

Any characteristic for which the applicant scores below the neutral score is then a potential reason for decline, since the probability of being bad based on this characteristic is more than 50% (note, at WOE = 0, the probability of being good or bad is 50%). An example of how one applicant scored on a scorecard is shown in Exhibit 6.16. The exhibit also provides the neutral score for this scorecard.

| EXHIBIT 6.16 | REASONS FOR DECLINE WITH NEUTRAL SCORE |

Scorecard	
Age	56
Time at Address	43
Postal Code	22
Inquiries 3 Mths	20
% Trades Delinquent	43
Oldest Trade	68
Debt Service Ratio	42
Utilization	25
Worst Rating	30
Neutral Score	31

Based on this applicant's scores, his top three reasons for decline would be Inquiries 3 Months, Postal Code, and Utilization. These are the three lowest-scoring characteristics below the neutral score.

Some institutions also calculate the "neutral score" based on the weighted average score of each attribute. An example of the weighted average calculation for "Time at Residence" is shown in Exhibit 6.17.

The weighted average is calculated using the formula:

$$\sum_{i=1}^{n} (\text{Distribution}_i * \text{score}_i)$$

The adverse code is then generated using attributes where the applicant scores below the calculated weighted average score. Ranking in this case can be done by calculating the percentage difference between the applicant's score and the weighted average, for all characteristics where the applicant has scored below the weighted average—the three biggest variances would then become the top three reasons for decline.

Points Allocation

Once the final scorecard is produced, the points allocation for each attribute, and the overall strength of the scorecard, should be checked. The allocation of scores needs to be logical, following trends established in the initial characteristic analysis. An example of score allocations from two separately developed scorecards is shown for "age" in Exhibit 6.18.

Scorecard 1 has a logical distribution; as age increases, applicants are given more points. This fits in well with the attribute weight distribution and with business experience. Scorecard 2, however, contains a

EXHIBIT 6.17   NEUTRAL SCORE USING WEIGHTED AVERAGE APPROACH

Time at Res	Distribution	Score	D x S
0–6	18%	12	2.16
7–18	32%	25	8
19–36	26%	28	7.28
37+	24%	40	9.6
Weighted Average			**27.04**

EXHIBIT 6.18	LOGICAL DISTRIBUTION OF POINTS ALLOCATION		

Age	Weight	Scorecard 1	Scorecard 2
Missing	−55.50	16	16
18–22	−108.41	12	12
23–26	−72.04	18	18
27–29	−3.95	26	14
30–35	70.77	35	38
35–44	122.04	43	44
44+	165.51	51	52

reversal at attribute "27–29." This could have been caused by correlation or some quirk in the sample data. This also happens when two groups have weights that are not sufficiently far apart. Note that if the approach outlined in this book is followed, with logical grouping and regression using WOE, this sort of reversal will not happen. These tend to occur where the raw data is used as an input into regression, and then the scores are assigned using other methods. Since this is the only reversal in this characteristic, and the rest of the points allocation is logical, a judgmental alteration of the points allocation is normally performed. Depending on the severity of the reversal, and the order of the points allocation for the rest of the attributes, regrouping characteristics and a revision of the stepwise regression may be needed.

This exercise becomes an iterative process until a statistically and operationally acceptable scorecard is produced.

CHOOSING A SCORECARD

Most Scorecard Developers would produce at least two or three different scorecards as part of any project. Developing several different scorecards becomes an easier option given the amount of control and flexibility associated with the development method shown in this book. Choosing a final scorecard from among these involves answering two questions, namely: Which scorecard is the best? and, How good is the scorecard? The questions are answered using a combination of statistical and business measures.

Misclassification

Scorecards are designed to predict the probability of a case being good or bad. More importantly, as predictive models, they are used for differentiating between good and bad cases. Misclassification statistics are a good way to determine whether a scorecard is providing the right differentiation. For operational purposes, companies normally choose a minimum level of acceptable bad rate (based on a score) as a "cutoff." Applicants scoring below the cutoff are declined for credit or services, or tagged as potential frauds. As a result, there is always a chance that an actual good may be classified as bad and therefore rejected, and vice versa. The same is true for behavior scorecards where a cutoff is used to decide positive or negative actions on certain accounts. To ensure better customer service, the final scorecard here needs to be chosen such that the level of such misclassification is minimized.

There are several measures used to gauge the level of such misclassification, and compare different scorecards. These measures compare the number of true goods and bads with the number of predicted goods and bads for a certain cutoff. "Goods" and "Bads" here refer to cases above and below the proposed cutoff.

The measures are based on a confusion (or misclassification) matrix, as illustrated in Exhibit 6.19.

A better scorecard would be one where the "true" cases are maximized, and conversely, "false" cases minimized. There are four main measures used to gauge misclassification:

Accuracy: (true positives and negatives) / (total cases)
Error rate: (false positives and negatives) / (total cases)
Sensitivity: (true positives) / (total actual positives)
Specificity: (true negatives) / (total actual negatives)

EXHIBIT 6.19   CONFUSION MATRIX

| | | Predicted | |
		Good	Bad
Actual	Good	True Positive	False Negative
	Bad	False Positive	True Negative

These statistics can be interpreted in business terms:

- False Positive—Acceptance of bads
- True Positive—Acceptance of goods
- False negative—Decline goods
- True Negative—Decline bads

Based on these measures, a company can then decide, for example, to maximize the rejection of bads. In this case, typically where the scorecards are being built to reduce losses, it would choose the scorecard that maximizes specificity. In the case where the company wishes to get higher market share and does not mind approving some bads, it can minimize the rejection of goods by choosing the scorecard that maximizes sensitivity. The statistics here are therefore being used in the context of the business goals for which the scorecard is being developed. This should reinforce the importance of deciding on an objective for scorecard development, as was discussed under the "Create Business Plan" section of Chapter 3.

Where several models have been developed for comparison, these statistics should be generated for each one, based on similar cutoffs (e.g., based on 70% final approval rate or 5% bad rate).

Note that where the scorecard has been developed without adjusting for oversampling, the misclassification matrix numbers need to be adjusted to reflect proper counts. This is done by multiplying cell counts by sample weights π_1 and π_2, as shown in Exhibit 6.20.

Scorecard Strength

Scorecard strength is the statistical measure of scorecard predictiveness. Most of the measures commonly used in the industry are for comparative purposes, and not absolute. These measures are normally used in conjunction with misclassification measures, as detailed in the previous section, and strategic considerations to select the final preferred scorecard.

In some cases, previously used or current scorecards are compared

EXHIBIT 6.20 CONFUSION MATRIX NUMBERS FOR UNADJUSTED SAMPLES

		Predicted	
		Good	Bad
Actual	Good	$n*(\text{True } P_s/\text{Actual } P_s)* \pi_1$	$n*(1 - \text{Sens})* \pi_1$
	Bad	$n*(1 - \text{Spec})* \pi_0$	$n*(\text{Spec})* \pi_0$

against new ones being built. One should be careful of such comparisons, as changes in data, applicant profiles, and marketing strategies may make these comparisons irrelevant or weak at best. For example, if the current scorecard has become unstable and unusable, it would not be relevant to compare, for example, the KS of this scorecard with the old one when it was developed. Scorecards should always be developed on a "best efforts" basis given the data. Some companies go back into history and use both the new and existing scorecards to score a group of accounts, and then track the performance of both scorecards. Again, if the current scorecard is not stable, this exercise is completely irrelevant to the current circumstances. Should there be a need to benchmark the current model, a better way would be to develop models using several approaches using the same data. For example, one could build scorecards using logistic regression with grouped variables, logistic regression with raw data, neural network, and a decision tree, and then compare the predictive power of each. This way, the strength or weakness of the preferred method and model would be better indicated.

Examples of methods used to compare scorecard predictive power include statistics such as:

- **AIC (Akaike's Information Criterion).** Penalizes for adding parameters to the model. Small values of AIC are preferred.
- **SBC (Schwarz's Bayesian Criterion).** The SBC also penalizes for adding parameters to the model. Small values of SBC are preferred. In the case of "risk profile" scorecards built using the methods described in this book, the SBC and AIC may not be the best methods to gauge strength, since here a premium has been

placed on having a broad-based scorecard rather than one with the absolute minimum characteristics.

- **Kolmogorov-Smirnov (KS).** This measures the maximum vertical separation (deviation) between the cumulative distributions of goods and bads. The weakness of this method is that the separation is measured only at the one point (which may not be around the expected cutoff point), and not on the entire score range. If the intended scorecard cutoff is at the upper or lower range of scores, this method may not provide a good indication of scorecard comparison. In such cases, it might be better to compare the deviation at the intended cutoff, since that is where maximum separation is most required. Exhibit 6.21 shows a sample KS calculation for two scorecards where the maximum KS measures occur at scores of 205 and 215, respectively. Scorecard "A" is stronger than scorecard "B" since "A" has a maximum deviation of about 41% compared to about 15% for Scorecard "B."

- **c-statistic.** This is the most powerful nonparametric two-sample test, and the measure is equivalent to the area under the Receiver

EXHIBIT 6.21   KOLGOMOROV-SMIRNOFF

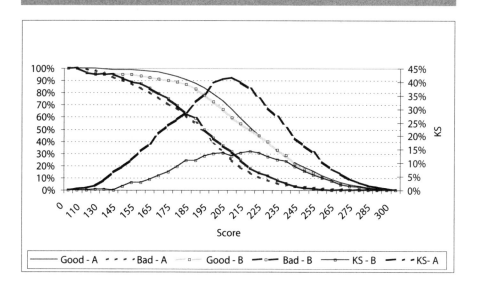

Operating Characteristic (ROC) curve, Gini coefficient, and the Wilcoxon-Mann-Whitney[8] test. It measures classifier performance across all score ranges and is a better measure of overall scorecard strength. The c-statistic measures the area under the *Sensitivity vs. (1 − Specificity)* curve for the entire score range. An example of a scorecard comparison using the c-statistic is given in Exhibit 6.22—where Scorecard "A" is stronger, as it has a higher area under its ROC curve than Scorecard "B."

The "random" line denotes c-statistic = 0.5. Therefore for a scorecard to be better than random selection, the c-statistic must be above 0.5. In most cases where good data is being used, a c-statistic of 0.7 and above would be considered adequate.

In some scorecard development solutions, such as SAS Credit Scoring, this statistic is automatically generated. The code shown in Exhibit 6.23 shows an example of some SAS code[9] that can be written to calculate the c-statistic.

- **Lorenz Curve.** A measure similar to the ROC curve used in the industry to compare models is to plot the distribution of "bad"

EXHIBIT 6.22   ROC CURVE

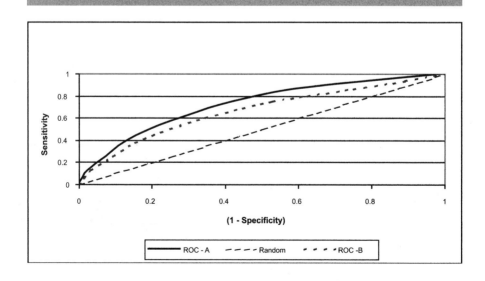

EXHIBIT 6.23   SAS CODE TO CALCULATE C-STATISTIC

```
proc rank data=&_VALID out=rscored;
  var PREDICTIONVARIABLE;
run;

proc sql;
  select sum(TARGET=1) as n1,
      (sum(PREDICTIONVARIABLE*(TARGETVARIABLE=1))-.5*(calculated
n1)*(calculated n1+1))
      /((calculated n1)*(count(TARGETVARIABLE)-(calculated n1)))
  as c
      from rscored;
quit;
```

cases and total cases by deciles across all score ranges. This is referred to as the Lorenz curve, and measures how well a scorecard isolates the bads and goods into selected deciles. An example of a Lorenz curve is shown in Exhibit 6.24.

In Exhibit 6.24, for the bottom 60% of the total sample, Scorecard "A" isolates about 90% of all bads, whereas scorecard "B" only isolates about 80%. Therefore, scorecard "A" displays stronger performance. Note that the ratio of the area between a scorecard's Lorenz curve and the 45 degree line, to the entire triangular area under the 45 degree line, is also equivalent to the Gini index.

It is important here to compare scorecard performance in operationally logical deciles, meaning that if the expected approval rate is about 60%, then performance should be compared at the 60% percentile mark. Comparing performance at the lowest 10% is irrelevant when what is needed at implementation is best performance, at 60% in this case. However, when dealing with scorecards such as bankruptcy or response, making comparisons at the lowest percentiles does make sense and should be done—since in these cases the objective is to isolate the worst/best few performers for action.

EXHIBIT 6.24   LORENZ CURVE

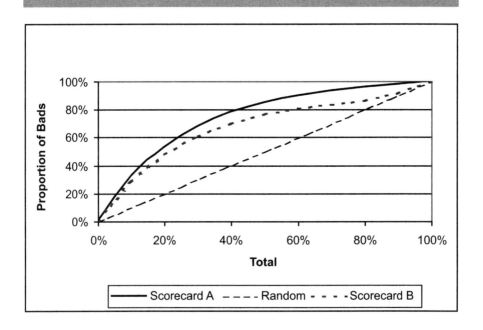

As with other decisions that have been made during the scorecard development process, the one to select a final scorecard should also be made with the objectives for scorecard development in mind. This may call for further analysis to determine which scorecard, for example, maximizes profit or minimizes false positives (for fraud scorecards), at a chosen cutoff. The objective is to first choose the scorecard that best helps the company achieve its strategic objectives, and then confirm that it has an acceptable statistical strength.

There are various other measures available to gauge scorecard strength, including:

- **Gains Chart.** Cumulative positive predicted value vs. distribution of predicted positives (*depth*).

- **Lift/Concentration Curve.** Sensitivity vs. depth.

$$\text{Lift} = \frac{\text{Positive predicted value}}{\% \text{ positives in the sample}}$$

- **Misclassification Costs.** Where losses are assigned to false positive and false negative cases. The optimal decision rule minimizes the total expected cost.[10]

- **Bayes Rule.** This minimizes expected cost (i.e., total misclassification cost). Bayes' rule and misclassification costs are difficult to implement in practice, due to problems in obtaining accurate loss numbers.

- **Cost Ratio.** Cost ratio is the ratio of the cost of misclassifying a bad credit risk as a good risk (false negative) to the cost of misclassifying a good risk as a bad (false positive). When used to calculate the cutoff, the cost ratio tends to max the sum of the two proportions of correct classification. This is done by plotting the cost ratio against sensitivity and specificity. The point where the two curves meet tends to be the point where both sensitivity and specificity are maximized.

- **Somers' D, Gamma, Tau-a.** Based on the numbers of concordant and discordant pairs. These measures are related to the c-statistic.

VALIDATION

Once the final scorecard has been selected, the results of the modeling need to be validated. Validation is performed to confirm that the model developed is applicable to the subject population, and to ensure that the model has not been overfitted. As mentioned earlier, it is recommended that the modeling be performed with a random 70% or 80% of the development sample, while the remaining 30% or 20% "holdout sample" be kept for validation. If the scorecard is being developed on a small sample, it may be necessary to develop it on 100% of the sample, and validate on several randomly selected 50% to 80% samples.

The first validation method is to compare the distributions of scored goods and bads across the two samples. Exhibit 6.25 shows an example of validation done on a holdout sample of 20%, and compared to the development sample.

EXHIBIT 6.25   VALIDATION CHART

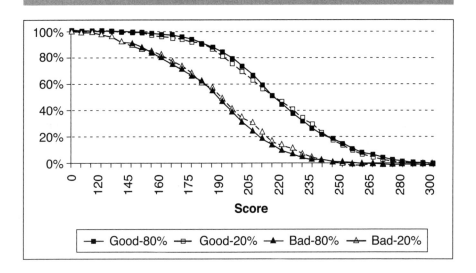

The scorecard is deemed validated if the two sets of data are not significantly different. Usually, a visual examination of the two curves is sufficient for this purpose. However, any goodness of fit measure such as Least Squares method or the information value can also be utilized.

A second method of validation is to compare development statistics for the development and validation samples. An example is given in Exhibit 6.26.

The scorecard is deemed validated where there is no significant difference between statistics for the two samples.

A further method to perform validation is to compare the divergence statistic for the development and validation holdout samples. Divergence can be calculated using the formula:

NOTE:

A further preimplementation validation is also conducted separately to confirm that the recent applicant profile is similar to that of the development sample. This will be discussed later in Chapter 8.

$$\text{Divergence} = (mean_G - mean_B)^2 / [\ 0.5\ (var_G + var_B)\ ]$$

where $mean_G$, $mean_B$, var_G, and var_B are the means and variances of the scored good and bad populations respectively.

Validation can also be performed by comparing the good/bad ratio by score range for the development and validation samples. If there is no significant difference in the bad rates by score for the two populations, the scorecard is deemed validated.

Significant differences in any of the preceding methods will require further analysis. Typically, characteristics with large score ranges present problems, since a small shift in the population distribution can cause a significant shift in scores. The same is true for scorecards developed with small samples and those developed on nonrandom samples. These are in addition to bad model development, where the characteristics selected for the model have overfit the data.

EXHIBIT 6.26   VALIDATION BY COMPARING PERFORMANCE STATISTICS

Fit Statistic	Label	Development	Validation
AIC	Akaike's Information Criterion	6214.0279153	.
ASE	Average Squared Error	0.0301553132	0.0309774947
AVERR	Average Error Function	0.1312675287	0.1355474611
DFE	Degrees of Freedom for Error	23609	.
DFM	Model Degrees of Freedom	7	.
DFT	Total Degrees of Freedom	23616	.
DIV	Divisor for ASE	47232	45768
ERR	Error Function	6200.0279153	6203.7361993
FPE	Final Prediction Error	0.0301731951	.
MAX	Maximum Absolute Error	0.9962871546	0.9959395534
MSE	Mean Square Error	0.0301642541	0.0309774947
NOBS	Sum of Frequencies	23616	22884
_NW_	Number of Estimate Weights	7	.
RASE	Root Average Sum of Squares	0.1736528525	0.1760042464
RFPE	Root Final Prediction Error	0.1737043324	.
RMSE	Root Mean Squared Error	0.1736785944	0.1760042464
SBC	Schwarz's Bayesian Criterion	6270.5156734	.
SSE	Sum of Squared Errors	1424.295752	1417.777979
SUMW	Sum of Case Weights Times Freq	47232	45768
MISC	Misclassification Rate	0.0320121951	0.0325117986
PROF	Total Profit for GB	3430000	2730000
APROF	Average Profit for GB	145.24051491	119.29732564

ENDNOTES

1. SAS Institute Inc. 1990. *SAS Procedures Guide*, version 6, first edition. Cary, NC: SAS Institute.

2. Kent Leahy. "Multicollinearity: When the Solution Is the Problem." in O. P. Rud. 2001. *Data Mining Cookbook*. Hoboken, NJ: John Wiley & Sons.

3. S. Kulback. 1959. *Information Theory and Statistics*. Hoboken, NJ: John Wiley & Sons.

4. SAS Institute Inc. 2004. *SAS 9.1.3 Help and Documentation*. Cary, NC: SAS Institute.

5. Ibid.

6. G. G. Chandler and J. Y. Coffman. 1977. "Using Credit Scoring to Improve the Quality of Consumer Receivables; Legal and Statistical Implications." Paper presented at the Financial Management Association meetings, Seattle, Washington.

7. G. J. McLachlan. 1975. "Iterative Reclassification Procedure for Constructing an Asymptotically Optimal Rule of Allocation in Discriminant Analysis." *Journal of American Statistical Association* 70, 365–369.

8. D. J. Hand. 1997. *Construction and Assessment of Classification Rules*. Hoboken, NJ: John Wiley & Sons.

9. W. J. E. Potts and M. J. Patetta. 2001. *Predictive Modeling Using Logistic Regression: Course Notes*. Cary, NC: SAS Institute.

10. G. J. McLachlan. 1992. *Discriminant Analysis and Statistical Pattern Recognition*. Hoboken, NJ: John Wiley & Sons; B. D. Ripley. 1996. *Pattern Recognition and Neural Networks*. Cambridge, UK: Cambridge University Press; D. J. Hand. *Construction and Assessment of Classification Rules*.

CHAPTER 7

Scorecard Development Process, Stage 5: Scorecard Management Reports

Once the final scorecard is selected, a full suite of management reports is produced. These reports are management tools, used for making operational decisions such as deciding the scorecard cutoff, designing account acquisition and management strategies, and monitoring future scorecard performance. These reports should be designed and produced to help the business user answer questions such as: "Where should I set my cutoff to meet my objectives?" and "What impact will that have on my portfolio?" Therefore, a good practice is to get the end users' input on what reports they would find useful for making decisions, and use that as a guide for producing reports.

These typically include development score and scorecard characteristics distributions, expected bad/approval rate charts, and the effects of the scorecard on key subpopulations. These scorecard management reports are run on the scorecard development dataset, including indeterminates and inferred rejects where appropriate.

In addition to these management reports, scorecard documentation should be produced detailing the analyses performed at each key phase of the project (i.e., business case development, definitions of good/bad/indeterminate, exclusions, segmentation, sampling and data gathering, initial characteristic analysis, model development, reject inference, scorecard performance statistics, and validation), and the output generated. This serves as reference material for future scorecard developments, audit and compliance requirements, future employees, and troubleshooting, should scorecard problems arise.

GAINS TABLE

A gains table includes a distribution of total, good, and bad cases by individual scores or score ranges. An example of a section from a gains table, using individual scores, is shown in Exhibit 7.1.

Gains tables are produced for the overall sample as well as for selected subpopulations. The key information in this table is:

- The expected bad rates for each score or score range (i.e., interval or marginal bad rate)
- The expected bad rates for all applicants above a certain score (i.e., cumulative bad rate)
- Expected approval rates at each score

This information is used in conjunction with financial and operational considerations to make cutoff decisions—that is, based on an expected bad rate or approval rate, at what cutoff should new applicants be approved? The objective of producing gains tables for subpopulations is to identify any abnormal effects on critical segments of business; for example, typically, scorecards developed on a mature population will penalize younger clients (a case for segmented scorecards). Typical subpopulations can include geographical, source of business, age, existing/new customers, segments to be targeted in future campaigns, and so forth.

EXHIBIT 7.1   SECTION OF A GAINS TABLE

Score	Count	Cumulative Count	Goods	Bads	Cumulative Goods	Cumulative Bads	Interval Bad Rate	Cumulative Bad Rate	Approval Rate
210	345	6,965	311	34	6,538	427	9.86%	6.13%	69.50%
211	500	6,620	462	38	6,227	393	7.60%	5.94%	66.20%
212	450	6,120	418	32	5,765	355	7.11%	5.80%	61.20%
213	345	5,670	323	22	5,347	323	6.38%	5.70%	56.70%

The distribution of the sample population by score is also used as a basis for scorecard stability and final score reports used for scorecard monitoring (which will be covered in Chapter 9).

CHARACTERISTIC REPORTS

These reports provide distributions for each characteristic included in the scorecard, as well as the approval rate and bad rate for each attribute by score. An example of a characteristic report is shown in Exhibit 7.2.

The upper part of the exhibit is used as a basis for characteristic analysis reports (see Chapter 9) performed as part of regular scorecard monitoring. The lower part is used to determine the effects of any proposed cutoff on the population by scorecard attributes, as well as segments deemed valuable to the organization. In Exhibit 7.2, if the cutoff is set at 212, only 58% of people aged 18–22 will be approved, compared to a 92% approval rate for people aged 44 and above. This may be acceptable to some organizations, but perhaps not to one looking to attract younger applicants. Similar reports produced to show the expected bad rate for each segment, by cutoff score, will alert business users to any overly risky subpopulation being approved. Options for such a scenario would be to try to develop a segmented scorecard for younger applicants, to maximize performance in that segment, or to use the same scorecard with different cutoffs for different segments.

EXHIBIT 7.2   CHARACTERISTIC REPORT

Age	Distr	Points	Bad Rate					
Missing	8%	16	16%					
18–22	9%	12	24%					
23–26	15%	18	18%					
27–29	26%	26	10%					
30–35	10%	35	5%					
35–44	20%	43	3%					
44 +	12%	51	2%					

Score	Missing	18–22	23–26	27–29	30–35	35–44	44 +
210	74%	70%	78%	80%	83%	91%	97%
211	67%	64%	71%	77%	80%	88%	95%
212	61%	58%	66%	70%	76%	84%	92%
213	56%	50%	61%	67%	72%	80%	87%

A variant of the characteristic report—in which distribution at development, and acceptance rate by segments are generated for characteristics not included in the scorecard—is also strongly recommended. These characteristics should be chosen to represent key subpopulations or target markets, to gauge the effects of any cutoffs on a particular segment in more detail. Such reports can be used to customize strategy for each segment, including setting different cutoffs for each.

The production of these reports typically marks the end of the scorecard development project. The next chapters will deal with how these scorecards are implemented and used for decision making.

CHAPTER 8

Scorecard Development Process, Stage 6: Scorecard Implementation

This section deals with postdevelopment analyses and will cover three main areas:

1. Understanding the analyses and business considerations in implementing risk scorecards.
2. Understanding how scorecards and management reports are used.
3. Understanding how strategy is developed.

PREIMPLEMENTATION VALIDATION

Preimplementation activities after scorecard development include testing for scoring accuracy and front-end validation. This validation exercise is similar to the one performed as part of scorecard development, but with different objectives. Whereas the objective previously was to confirm the robustness of the scorecard by comparing distributions of development and validation datasets, the objective here is to confirm that the scorecard developed is valid for the current applicant population. In some cases where the development sample is two or three years old, significant shifts in applicant profile may have occurred, and need to be identified. The results of this validation are also used as part of the analysis to set cutoffs.

Before the validation can be performed, all new external and internal scorecard characteristics need to be programmed into external data interfaces (e.g., credit bureau) as well as into the application processing and decision-making systems so that these characteristics can be used for scoring.

Once all the characteristics have been programmed, accuracy testing of the scorecard can be done. Validation reports can be produced as part of the accuracy testing to make the process more efficient. Ideally, testing should be done in the same environment where the scorecard is to be implemented (i.e., in test regions of the production system). If the test area is not available, programs in, for example, SAS code need to be written to simulate scoring and generate population distributions. This, however, does not give an accurate representation of how the actual production system will interpret the various scoring characteristics, especially calculated ones, and may lead to inaccurate forecasts. It is therefore essential that the accuracy testing be as closely aligned with actual production conditions as possible.

Once scoring accuracy has been established, front-end validation reports can be generated by scoring recent applications using the new scorecard, and comparing their distributions with that of the development sample. Usually scoring only the most recent batch of applications is done for this. However, it is good practice to do this analysis for several recent time periods where data is available (e.g., last month, last three months, last six months, and so on) in order to detect any emerging trends, or to confirm that deviations in one particular month do not represent any long-term trend.

Typically, system stability and characteristic analysis reports are produced for this. These reports can be generated both for application and behavior scorecards.

System Stability Report

An example of a system stability report is shown in Exhibit 8.1. Note that the system stability report is also sometimes referred to as the population stability or scorecard stability report.

EXHIBIT 8.1   SYSTEM STABILITY REPORT

Score Range	Actual %	Expected %	(A-E)	A/E	ln(A/E)	Index
0–169	7%	8%	−1%	0.8750	−0.1335	0.0013
170–179	8%	10%	−2%	0.8000	−0.2231	0.0045
180–189	7%	9%	−2%	0.7778	−0.2513	0.0050
190–199	9%	13%	−4%	0.6923	−0.3677	0.0147
200–209	11%	11%	0%	1.0000	0.0000	0.0000
210–219	11%	10%	1%	1.1000	0.0953	0.0010
220–229	10%	9%	1%	1.1111	0.1054	0.0011
230–239	12%	10%	2%	1.2000	0.1823	0.0036
240–249	11%	11%	0%	1.0000	0.0000	0.0000
250+	14%	9%	5%	1.5556	0.4418	0.0221

Index =   0.05327824

The "Actual %" and "Expected %" columns denote the distribution of cases for recent and development samples, respectively, for each of the score ranges specified.

The index as shown measures the magnitude of the population shift between recent applicants and expected (from development sample). This index is calculated as:

$$\sum (\% \text{ Actual} - \% \text{ Expected}) \times ln\ (\% \text{ Actual} / \% \text{ Expected})$$

for all score ranges.

In general, an index of less than 0.10 shows no significant change, 0.10–0.25 denotes a small change that needs to be investigated, and an index greater than 0.25 points to a significant shift in the applicant population.

Other methods, such as Chi Square with some level of significance, may also be used to measure the magnitude of the shift. The method shown in Exhibit 8.1 is one used widely in the industry.

A further way to confirm the nature of the population shift is to view a graph of the current versus expected applicant distributions by score. This can provide additional information (e.g., whether the shift in scores is downward, upward, or kurtosis).

The index above is not an end-all measure. Factors such as trends (Is the change a temporary occurrence or something more long-term?), magnitude of the shift, and reasons for change should also be taken into account before deciding if a population shift is significant.

Shifts in scores can be due to several reasons:

- Independent change in applicant profile (e.g., demographic change).
- Marketing campaigns, niche competition, and so forth. For example, if the recent month's applicants were noticeably younger or were concentrated in a particular area, this may be due to focused marketing activity. Changes in product, such as the addition of loyalty programs, changes in fee structure, "no interest for six months"–type sweeteners, or shift to nontraditional channels, can also attract a different type of applicant. External competition, particularly from new entrants into the market who target a narrow demographic—such as monoline credit card companies who target professionals—may also affect the makeup of your applicants. In behavior scoring, more aggressive authorizations or credit line management strategies, introduction of loyalty programs, repricing, cross-selling, and other such activities can change the profile of existing customers.
- Error in coding. This is typically a systematic error.
- Mistakes in data capture, whereby the data represents a nonrandom or incorrectly segmented sample, or exclusions from the development sample are included.

A point to note is that for a pure system stability report, the applicant population must be generated using the same exclusion criteria as the development sample. Companies, however, perform a second set of analyses for the scorecard cutoff in which all applicants are included. This is to provide a more realistic analysis of the expected approval rate, and of the effects of the cutoff on key segments.

The system stability report only indicates whether a shift has occurred, and gives an indication of the magnitude. For business decision making, finding out the source of the population shift is far more important, since only that allows remedial actions to be taken where necessary.

Further investigation to pinpoint the cause of the shift can be done through:

- Performing a characteristic analysis to analyze shifts in scorecard characteristics
- Analyzing shifts in nonscorecard characteristics that are believed to have an impact on the applicant quality and those that can explain underlying reasons for scorecard characteristic shifts (more on this in the next section)
- Gathering information on recent marketing campaigns and other initiatives

Characteristic Analysis Report

The characteristic analysis report provides information on the shifts in the distribution of scorecard (and other) characteristics, and the impact on the scores due to that shift. An example of a characteristic analysis for "Age" is shown in Exhibit 8.2.

"Expected %" and "Actual %" again refer to the distributions of the development and recent samples, respectively. The index here is calculated simply by:

$$\sum (\% \text{ Actual} - \% \text{ Expected}) \times (\text{Points})$$

for all score ranges.

Exhibit 8.2 shows a shift toward a younger applicant, resulting in applicants scoring about 2.63 points less than at development for age.

EXHIBIT 8.2   CHARACTERISTIC ANALYSIS

Age	Expected %	Actual %	Points	Index
18–24	12%	21%	10	0.9
25–29	19%	25%	15	0.9
30–37	32%	28%	25	−1
38–45	12%	6%	28	−1.68
46+	25%	20%	35	−1.75
				−2.63

140   SCORECARD DEVELOPMENT PROCESS, STAGE 6

Analyses on all the scorecard characteristics are done in the same fashion to more comprehensively pinpoint the reasons for score shifts.

Similar analyses to compare development versus current distributions are performed for other characteristics, including:

- Characteristics that are not in the scorecard, but are believed to have an impact on applicant quality. These include strong characteristics that did not make it into the scorecard. For example, if shifts in the scorecard characteristics point to a deteriorating quality of applicants, reviewing these strong nonscorecard characteristics will help to confirm that movement. This ensures that judgments on applicant quality are made with a wider variety of information and therefore more robust.

- Characteristics that are similar to the ones in the scorecard. For example, if "age" is in the scorecard, tracking other time-related characteristics—such as time at employment or address, and age of oldest trade—may explain further reasons for the shift in applicant profile. If "inquiries in the last 6 months" is in the scorecard, tracking inquiries in the last three and twelve months will help to further explain the shift in inquiries. Related characteristics should all move in the same direction (e.g., older applicants should have higher tenures at work or older files at the bureau). Examples of other information types for which this can be done include trades, demographics, inquiries, and financial ratios.

- Where ratios are used in the scorecard, distributions of the denominator and numerator should also be tracked to explain changes in the ratio itself. For example, if utilization (balance divided by credit limit) has decreased, it may be due to either balances moving lower or credit limits being increased.

Again, these analyses should be performed to compare development data with recent historical data over the last one to six months, to detect any trends and to validate that the shifts in distributions are not a temporary phenomenon.

The shifts in scored and nonscored characteristics should be consistent and explainable using logic and business considerations. If, for example, analysis shows that applicants are getting younger, yet have higher "time at employment," coding errors may be occurring. Such illogical shifts must be investigated and explained.

What if the Scorecard Does Not Validate?

If analysis shows that the population has shifted significantly, the user is left with a few options. Redeveloping the scorecard may not be a viable choice, since the data sample for this redevelopment will likely come from the same time period as the original scorecard, which did not validate. In such cases, users can adjust their applicant population expectations based on the new distributions and further adjust cutoff and other strategies accordingly. This means regenerating the scorecard management reports, as outlined in the previous section, with new total distribution numbers, but keeping the odds relationship at each score the same. Based on qualitative and quantitative analyses, the bad rate expectations can then be changed as well. For example, if it is deemed that the population is of lower quality than expected, conservative measures can be taken to increase "bad rate" expectations and loan/credit line amounts can be lowered at the margins.

The qualitative analysis to be done at this point is based on the reasons for shifts in scores. For example, if all analyses point to a younger applicant with higher levels of delinquency and less stability, the expected performance is obvious. In some cases, the shifts may be less so. For example, cases where "credit line utilization" has generally gone down denote lower risk. This could be due to a decline in balances (which truly shows lowered risk), or to an increase in available credit limits due to competitive pressure among banks (which may not be indicative of lowered risk). Understanding such reasons for score shifts will assist in making an educated evaluation of the expected performance.

If the reasons for score shifts are well understood, changes to score points assigned can also be attempted. For example, where industry competition results in overall credit line increases, which artificially decreases utilization, fewer points can be assigned to people with lower utilization, to reflect a higher risk than what is suggested by the score-card. This is not something to be attempted without a thorough under-standing of the reasons for score points shift, and is only a "best fit" business solution to a problem. Another option is to isolate the reason for shift, and develop a separate scorecard for it. For example, the bank traditionally targeted people with established credit histories, but has recently started wooing those who are new debtors. The first step is, of course, to speak to Marketing or other departments to find this out. The portfolio can then be split into two segments, one for the estab-lished and the other for new debtors, and two separate scorecards devel-oped. Note that if the new debtor market is entirely new for the bank, it will need to get a generic scorecard to start with.

There are also statistical techniques available whereby the develop-ment sample distributions can be "adjusted" to be similar to more recent distributions. However, this only adjusts the characteristics, and may not represent the performance behavior of the original sample.

The preimplementation validation is complete once it is established that the scorecard is valid for the current applicant population. At this point, strategy development work can begin.

STRATEGY DEVELOPMENT

General Considerations

Scorecards are developed for certain business objectives. Once the scorecard is developed, the user needs to decide how it is to be used to attain those objectives. This involves performing analysis for, and mak-ing risk-adjusted decisions on, issues such as the minimum score for approval (cutoff), initial credit lines or automated credit line increases, setting conditions, establishing policy rules, and implementing "Challenger" strategies where appropriate. Typically, front-end valida-tion reports in conjunction with expected performance reports are used for this purpose.

Strategy development is decision making, and, as with all decision making, there are several general things one should bear in mind during strategy development:

- **Effects on Key Segments.** Any strategy implemented, or decision made, should be analyzed for its effects on key segments (e.g., regional, demographic, and distribution channel). "Key segments" refers especially to those segments deemed valuable to the company, or important target markets. This reduces the chances of surprises, and allows the company to take steps such as using the same scorecard, but with different cutoffs for certain segments. The importance of this analysis is even greater where separate scorecards have not been developed for these segments, and where the applicant profile varies significantly between segments (e.g., branch customer vs. Internet).

- **"What-if" Analysis.** Where companies are utilizing a decision-making engine, "what-if" analysis needs to be done for "Challenger" strategies. The purpose is to get an initial idea of the effects of the intended new strategy on the ongoing business, whether it will perform better than the existing "Champion" and the volume of accounts falling into each defined scenario. Again, the purpose is to make the most informed decision possible.

- **Policy Rules.** Implementation of new strategies gives the company an opportunity to revisit and enhance policy rules, especially when putting in new scorecards. Special attention needs to be paid to alignment of decisions based on scoring and policy rules, so that they do not negate each other, and the effectiveness of each can be tracked and evaluated independently.

Scoring Strategy

In environments where a single scorecard is being used for a segment, the scoring strategy is fairly simple. Each applicant, or customer, is scored using that scorecard and adjudicated based on a set cutoff. However, where multiple scorecards are being used, various methods are available. Multiple-scorecard usage occurs when, for example, an applicant is scored for delinquency, attrition, bankruptcy, and profitability, and when a credit bureau or other externally based scorecard is used to supplement the in-house model.

There are three main approaches to implementing a multiple scoring solution:

1. Sequential
2. Matrix
3. Matrix-sequential hybrid

Sequential　Using this method, the applicant is scored on each scorecard sequentially, with separate cutoffs. See Exhibit 8.3.

Exhibit 8.3 shows a sample sequential scoring flow where three scorecards are used to adjudicate each application. Note that in addition to "pass" and "fail," other decisions such as "refer" can also be used. However, this strategy is best implemented where absolute "hurdles" are being used—for example, applicant *must* pass a bankruptcy score or a minimum bureau score to be approved—and there are no gray areas. Where gray areas do exist (e.g., revenue scores), a matrix strategy is better.

Matrix　In the matrix scoring method, multiple scorecards are used concurrently with decision making based on a combination of the cutoffs for the various scorecards. The example in Exhibit 8.4 shows a matrix of expected risk and churn (or attrition), where gray areas have been established.

This approach is most frequently used where a balanced choice needs to be made from different types of, preferably independent, information. A good score from one scorecard may balance a bad score from another; for example, do you want to approve a low delinquency risk

EXHIBIT 8.3　　SEQUENTIAL SCORING

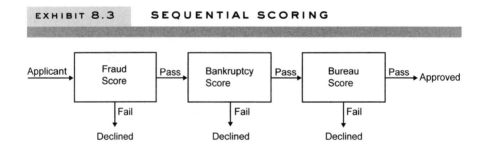

EXHIBIT 8.4   MATRIX SCORING

		Churn Score				
		0–549	550–619	620–649	650–699	700 +
In- House Delq Score	0–189	Decline		Refer		Decline
	190–209					
	210–229					
	230–249			Approve		
	250 +					

applicant who also has a high probability of attrition, or would you approve someone who is likely to be delinquent but has a low probability of rolling forward to write-off?

The example in Exhibit 8.4 shows:

- Applicants with a high delinquency score (denoting low risk) and a high churn score (denoting low probability of churn) being approved
- Applicants with low scores for both delinquency and churn being declined
- Applicants who are in the gray zone being referred for further scrutiny
- Applicants with a low delinquency score and a high churn score (i.e., they are high-risk and have a low probability of churning) being declined outright

The balance depends on in-house priorities and objectives. Common examples are custom in-house versus bureau scorecards (performance with the bank balanced by performance with other creditors), delinquency versus profitability, delinquency versus churn/attrition, and delinquency versus bankruptcy/chargeoff (to isolate accounts that have a tendency to become delinquent but eventually pay up). The key aspect to note is that both measures must be independent of each other and preferably be providing competing information.

In Exhibit 8.4, three separate zones have been created based on scores from both the in-house risk and revenue scorecards. Similarly, where appropriate, three-dimensional matrices can be designed for more sophisticated decision making.

Matrix-Sequential Hybrid   In some multiple-scorecard scenarios, a hybrid of the previously mentioned methods is used, whereby applicants are prequalified using a sequential approach, and then put through a matrix strategy. For example, applicants can be put through a bankruptcy model first, and upon passing the cutoff, be moved to a matrix strategy consisting of delinquency/profit/churn scores. This approach is simpler than a multidimensional matrix, and more versatile than sequential scoring. It is best used where more than three independent scorecards are being used, and can balance several competing interests. The hybrid strategy can also be used in conjunction with policy rules to prequalify applicants.

Setting Cutoffs

Most organizations that use scorecards set minimum score levels at which they are willing to accept applicants (or qualify them for any subsequent account treatment with behavior scorecards). This minimum score is referred to as a "cutoff," and can represent a threshold risk, profit, or some other level, depending on the organization's objectives in using the scorecard. A simple example of a cutoff strategy for new account acquisition is shown in Exhibit 8.5.

In this case, anyone who scores above 210 points using the scorecard is accepted automatically, anyone scoring below 190 is declined, and those scoring in between are referred to manual adjudication for further scrutiny. In account management cases, several cutoff points may exist for actions such as varying collections actions (from soft actions to more stringent ones) or for assigning increasingly higher credit limits. More sophisticated strategies can be developed for more complex applications in account acquisition, for example:

EXHIBIT 8.5   CUTOFF STRATEGY DECISIONS

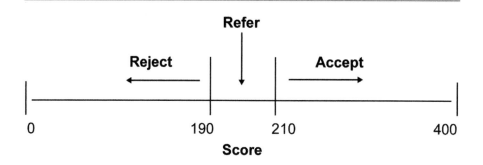

- Assigning different levels of "Accept," based on the level of due diligence or additional information needed to give final approval to an application—for example, pending appraisals for mortgage loans, or pending confirmation of income. In some cases, cutoffs are set above which income confirmation is not required. This reduces the workload for low-risk customers or for low-value loans. In addition, more stringent income confirmation methods, such as providing a copy of their pay stub to a branch, may be required of higher-risk applicants, whereas low-risk ones may be asked to simply fax theirs in.

- Assigning a "hard lowside cutoff" at a score below which overriding (overturning the scorecard decision) is not allowed. For example, a bank may have a final cutoff of 200 points for approval and may set a hard lowside cutoff of 180. This means that branch staff or adjudicators may override declined applications that score between 180 and 200, if they have good reason to do so. There is usually no "hard highside cutoff." Companies will always override applicants based on policy rules, and so forth, no matter how high they score.

Cutoff Analysis   A typical starting point for selecting a suitable cutoff for application scorecards is to analyze the relationship between expected approval and bad rates for different scores. These are only the two most basic considerations. Similar analysis can be done to gauge the impact of selecting a cutoff on "tradeoff" parameters such as profitability and revenue, bad rate and revenue, and other relevant metrics.

A good approach in balancing the tradeoff between bad rate and approval rate is to identify two key points in the score range:

1. The score cutoff that corresponds to maintaining the current approval rate (and yields the new expected bad rate); that is, answer the question "What will be my bad rate if I keep my approval rate the same?"

2. Conversely, the score cutoff that corresponds to maintaining the current bad rate (and yields the new expected approval rate); that is, answer the question "What will be my new approval rate if I keep my bad rate the same?"

In general, each new generation of scorecards developed should be better than the last, and the preceding analysis should yield results where the organization gets a lower bad rate for the same approval rate, or a higher approval rate while holding the bad rate constant.

Exhibit 8.6, a "tradeoff chart," plots the bad rate and approval rate across a selected range of scores, using numbers from the gains tables produced earlier. Note that the preceding analysis should be done using the most current applicant distributions (for approval rates), with expected bad rates from development. The exhibit shows an example for a company whose current bad rate is about 5% and approval rate 55%.

If the objective for developing scorecards is to increase market share, or if losses are not of concern, the company may choose to maintain its current bad rate levels by choosing a cutoff of 207, and achieve a new, higher approval rate of about 62%. This means that the organization can be more aggressive in approving more people, yet keep its risk exposure constant by doing a better job of selecting applicants for approval. Note that this occurs due to the presence of the "swap set," as discussed in the "Reject Inference" section of Chapter 6.

Conversely, if the objective for scorecard development is to reduce losses, the company may choose a cutoff of 213, maintaining its approval rate but gaining a lower expected bad rate of about 2.5%. This

EXHIBIT 8.6   TRADEOFF CHART

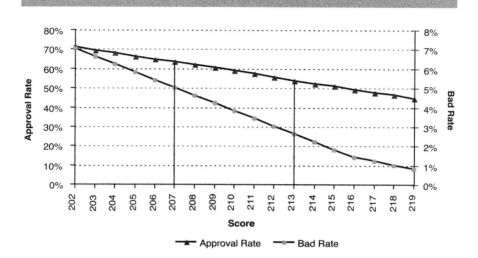

would mean that the company would reduce its risk exposure but take in the same number of new customers.

Where a specific objective exists, one of the above two options can be exercised. Typically, where there is no specific objective, companies choose cutoffs in between the two key cutoff points (207 and 213 in Exhibit 8.6), where there is both a gain in approval rate and a decrease in expected bad rate.

The choice of cutoff is not limited to between these two points (207 to 213 in Exhibit 8.6). Some choose to set a lower cutoff to get higher bad rates than current, but with the expectation of higher profitability. For example, a mortgage portfolio manager with losses in the single digit basis points may decide to lower the cutoff and increase his losses by a few more basis points, in the expectation of a higher market share and greater overall profitability.

Tradeoff charts like the one shown in Exhibit 8.6 can be plotted for other competing interests, depending on the objectives for developing scorecards, for example, risk/profit and risk/churn.

Gauging Impact   Once a preliminary cutoff is selected, its impact on key subpopulations and segments needs to be measured. Again, this is to ensure that all possible outcomes are anticipated before a final strategy is developed. Reports such as those in Exhibits 7.1 and 7.2 can be used to analyze expected approval rates and bad rates by scorecard criteria, as well as important segments. A sensible way to identify such segments is to refer to Marketing departments to identify future and current target markets, and to the segmentation analyses done earlier that will identify segments that were deemed different but do not yield sufficient data for scorecard development.

For behavior scoring, segments will comprise the groups of people who are likely to be targeted for actions such as collections, renewal, and credit line management.

These reports should be performed on recent samples of applicants to get a more accurate reflection of expected approval behavior.

It is strongly recommended that these reports be run especially where characteristics containing negative behavior (e.g., bankruptcy) are used. This is to align organizational expectations and prevent questions such as "How did this person with a bankruptcy get approved?" It is imperative that users understand that based on a chosen overall cutoff, there is a statistical chance that a certain proportion of people with bankruptcy will get approved. This proportion may be very small, depending on the cutoff and the scorecard's ability to isolate people with bankruptcies into the lower score ranges.

It must also be understood that if a cutoff decision has been made with an overall risk profile in mind, these applicants with bankruptcies must have scored high enough on other characteristics to reach the cutoff score. An example of such an analysis is shown in Exhibit 8.7.

The exhibit shows that in the range of cutoffs being considered, between 8% and 22% of previous bankrupts may be approved. The organization can then adjust the cutoff based on its comfort level. However, the only way to prevent all previous bankrupts from being approved is to apply a hard policy rule. If the organization has such rules, characteristics with bankruptcy information should not be used in scorecards, as application of the policy rule will create skewed results and undermine the performance of the scorecard. This must be understood at the outset when characteristics are being selected for inclusion into the scorecard (initial characteristic analysis).

EXHIBIT 8.7   APPROVAL RATE BY SCORE—WORST DELINQUENCY AT BUREAU

Score	Nvr Delq	30 days	60 days	90 days	120 days	Bankrupt
210	97%	70%	56%	50%	41%	22%
211	95%	62%	48%	41%	36%	18%
212	92%	58%	41%	38%	31%	12%
213	87%	50%	37%	31%	25%	8%

In the case where undesirable performance is detected for particular segments, the decision maker has some choices, including;

- Using the same scorecard, but with different cutoffs for different segments. For example, assume there are five regions in the country, with differing bad rates corresponding to the proposed overall cutoff. If the overall targeted bad rate is, for example, 2.5%, one can select the appropriate cutoff for each segment that would result in a predicted bad rate of 2.5% for each one. This way, the better segments would be rewarded with higher approval rates, while the riskier ones would be penalized, but with the overall portfolio loss goals intact. The analysis can be similarly done with approval rate targets in mind. The same mindset can be applied to behavior scores and strategies for credit line assignment or repricing.

- Redeveloping the scorecard with different characteristics.

- Adding policy rules to prevent certain segments from being approved, or to impose higher standards for some segments.

- Exploring further segmentations for segments being overpenalized or overrewarded. A significant deviation from "average" performance indicates the need for segmentation, especially if the segments in question are particularly important ones.

Strategy Development Communication

The importance of understanding the impact of strategies has been discussed in the previous section. A good practice is to get the various interested parties (mentioned in the "Scorecard Development Roles" section in Chapter 2) involved. These players can help in anticipating changes, and therefore preparing for it. Examples include:

- **Marketing.** This is a valuable source of information to identify key segments and better predict any impact on marketing initiatives. Marketing can also inform Risk Management of any ongoing marketing and other acquisition/account management campaigns that may be negatively impacted by introducing new scorecards and cutoffs, or that may explain shifts in applicant or account profiles (during preimplementation validation).

- **IT.** Expected changes may require involvement from IT, and increase lead times to implementation, especially if scorecards are changed, new scorecards developed, or multiple cutoff strategies adopted (with the corresponding increase in reports required). In addition, if scorecard scaling is changed, IT may be required to reprogram any hardcoded policy rules, strategies based on scores, and other interfaces used for decision making.

- **Adjudication/Authorizations.** Cutoff choices or policy rules that increase the number of "refer" cases may result in higher volumes going into branch or other adjudication centers. Similarly, more credit card transactions being pushed into manual authorizations will require more staffing in authorization centers to maintain reasonable customer service. In some cases where increased capacity is not an option, cutoff choices will have to be made with this constraint in mind.

- **Collections.** In some cases, a creditor may take additional risks that will increase the volume of cases going into collections. These can be reasonably forecasted, so that collections staff are better prepared in the future to handle the increased volumes. For example, a calculated risk may be taken where the approval rate is significantly increased (along with the expected bad rate), but with expectations of higher profitability. In this case, Collections departments may experience a significant volume increase that may require additional staff being hired. In addition, taking more losses (but with higher overall profit due to higher revenues) might be a good idea for the strategy department, but not for someone else who is compensated based on the amount of losses.

- **Finance.** Information required to calculate the profitability of new strategies typically comes from Finance departments.

- **Corporate Risk.** Higher credit lines will require more capital allocation; risk-based pricing may require changes to hedging. In come cases, overly aggressive strategies may not comply with corporate risk standards.

- **Customer Service.** Calculated negative impacts on various segments will need to be handled. For example, an ongoing campaign targeting a certain segment, who are asked to call in to apply for products, may be negatively impacted if that segment is discovered to be high-risk during scorecard development. In this case, the company may choose to provide written scripts to the customer service agents, and offer bonus reward points to customers who are declined, to minimize this impact. Similarly, if policy rules or cutoff changes are made that increase the volume of accounts or applications going into authorizations or adjudication centers, there may be an unacceptably long wait time for customers who want to make a purchase or who would like a decision on their application.

- **Education.** Staff may need to be retrained to understand new scorecard scaling, cutoffs, and strategies. Such education costs can be lowered by standardizing the scaling of scorecards across products and segments, such that new scores will mean the same as previous ones, and a score of, for example, 200 will mean the same across all scorecards. Another strategy to decrease education costs (and better preserve the confidentiality of scores) is to map scores to grades such as A, B, C, D, and so on. Each new scorecard development will only require the mapping changed at the source, instead of mass reeducation. Appropriate staff members will see the grade, not the score, and policy rules associated with each grade will not need to be changed.

- **Legal.** Analyzing the impact of cutoffs on certain geographical areas may allay fears of "redlining," and reduce the chances of the lender being accused of discriminatory practices.

Risk-Adjusted Actions

At this point, we have a cutoff and therefore know the risk level of marginal applicants and of those above the chosen cutoff (the approves). Strategy development uses this information to create risk-adjusted strategies or actions to maximize business objectives. These actions will differ based on products offered. Strategies can be developed for applicants or existing accounts—the objective of creating risk-adjusted decision making remains the same. For example, depending on score and other criteria, various strategies can be developed, such as:

- Risk-adjusted pricing for loans and other credit products, and insurance premiums for new accounts and also for repricing loans coming up for renewals.
- Offering product upgrades (e.g., gold card, platinum card) to better customers, or inviting them to apply for a lower interest rate card based on their risk.
- Setting the level of down payment/deposit for financed products such as auto loans and mortgages, or setting renewal terms.
- Cross-selling of other products to better customers through pre-approvals. Note that risk and propensity scores should always be used in conjunction with ability to service debt in cross-selling. This ensures that cross-sell offers are made to customers who not only will accept the offer and are at a lower risk of default, but also can cope with the additional credit.
- Giving higher line of credit or credit card limit to better customers, both at application and as an existing customer (see example in Exhibit 8.8).

EXHIBIT 8.8 CREDIT LINE STRATEGY

	Debt Service Ratio				
Score	0–10%	11–15%	16–24%	25–35%	36%+
230–234	$3,500	$3,500	$2,500	$2,500	$2,000
235–239	$4,000	$3,500	$3,000	$2,500	$2,000
240–244	$4,500	$4,000	$3,500	$3,000	$2,500
245–249	$5,000	$4,500	$4,000	$3,500	$3,000
250 +	$7,500	$5,000	$4,500	$4,000	$3,500

- Setting overall corporate exposure per customer based on the risk profile, to manage concentration risks.
- Using milder collection methods for low-risk customers (e.g., sending letters, using auto-dialers), and harsher actions for high-risk ones (e.g., sending to collection agency).
- Varying payments terms for commercial customers (i.e., better customers get more lenient terms, while high-risk ones are asked for payment before goods delivered).
- Allowing low-risk customers to make purchases on their credit cards above their limits, or when they are in early stages of delinquency.
- Investigation for fraudulent application (i.e., using fraud scores), or requiring full real estate appraisals for high-risk mortgages.

An example of a credit-limit-granting strategy for a credit card is shown in Exhibit 8.8.

The first thing to note is that this strategy is based on two independent and relevant measures. The risk score (on the left) measures likelihood of default on debt, and debt service ratio measures the proportion of a person's income being used to service debts (an indication of his or her ability to carry further debt). A lower debt service ratio is better, as it indicates that the person has more than sufficient income to make payments on the debt. The strategy shows customers with higher scores and lower debt service ratios getting higher credit limits. Once the measures to be used for determining credit line assignment are established, the user has various options to assign the actual credit line. Some examples include:

- Determine current line assignment practice based on the two measures, and then use consensus-based judgment to assign higher lines to the better customers and lower to the high-risk ones. For example, the top customers may get a 30% increase, and the worse ones a 30% decrease. Once the bottom left-hand (best) and the top right-hand (worst) boxes are filled, the rest can be filled in.

- Determine the maximum and minimum credit lines the creditor is willing to give, and assign these to the best and worst customers in the table. Fill in the rest based on incremental increases or decreases.

- Based on the total expected loss for a cohort, expected probability of default (*PD*), the loss given default (*LGD*), and the exposure at default (*EAD*) numbers, one can work backward to assign optimal maximum exposures (credit limit) for each cell in the matrix above. Some assumptions will need to be made for the distribution of expected loss for each cell. For simplicity, assume that the loss per account for a cell is $500. If the probability of default is 6% and the loss given default is 97% of the limit, then the maximum credit limit for this cell can be calculated based on:

$$\text{Expected loss} = EAD \times PD \times LGD$$
$$500 = EAD \times 0.05 \times 0.97$$
$$EAD = \$10,309$$

The objective of presenting these three choices is not to recommend definitive ways to assign credit lines. The first point here is that the choice of metrics to be used in decision making is key. Many organizations use risk score only to assign credit lines or loan amount. This only presents half the story. As Exhibit 8.8 shows, a balance between probability of repayment and ability to repay makes more sense. The second point is that for every decision, one needs to evaluate options from the simplest to the most complex. Sometimes the simplest options, such as the first two given above, are the best. The first two options are simple, justifiable, and based on two measures that make sense.

Policy Rules

Policy rules consist of a set of corporate guidelines designed to support the decision-making process. These include legal and risk-related rules such as minimum requirements and risk policies. Examples include:

- Legal age requirements (e.g., age < 18, then decline)
- Employment (e.g., if not employed, self-employed, or employed less than one year, then decline or refer)
- Bankruptcy (e.g., recent bankruptcy, or bankruptcy < two years ago, then refer or decline)
- Delinquency limits (e.g., more than three delinquencies at the bureau, then decline)
- Application type (e.g., VIP or staff application, then refer)
- Previous in-house record (e.g., previous at-fault claim or write-off, then refer)
- Minimum credit line for overrides or certain types of account (e.g., student or previous bankrupt)
- No credit line increase if one has been granted in the last six months

Policy rules are a necessary and prudent part of risk management. The important thing is that they should be based on independent and validated measures. They should also preferably not be based on score-card characteristics, so as not to undermine the scoring process. For example, if bankruptcy or previous delinquency is taken account of in the scorecard, then preferably these criteria should not be used in policy rules. In situations where the usage of such rules is critical, then it is better to build scorecards using other criteria.

Policy rules are also often judgmental, and are seldom tested empirically. Some policy rules exist merely because someone put them in years ago, and no one bothered to review them after that. Where possible, they should be reviewed, tested, and proven to be effective from time to time (e.g. annually). Credit scorecard development projects can sometimes confirm the effectiveness of some policy rules in the initial characteristic analysis phase. Note, however, that postinferred data should be used, so as to minimize the effects of cherry-picking, since some policy rules are used as blanket refusal policies.

Policy rules are most often used in the overriding process (i.e., reversing decisions made with the cutoff). As with strategies, they should be developed with input from operational, legal, and risk departments so as to ensure that all potential effects are addressed.

Overrides

Overrides refer to manual or automated decisions that reverse the one taken on the basis of score cutoffs (i.e., one that contradicts the decision recommended by the scorecard). This happens in new applicant scoring. There are two kinds of overrides:

1. **Lowside Overrides.** Applicants scoring below cutoff who are approved
2. **Highside Overrides.** Applicants scoring above cutoff who are declined

Overrides, like policy rules, are a necessary and prudent part of risk management, which need to be used properly. A general rule for overriding is that it should be done based on *significant information available independent of the scorecard*. Since scorecards are usually developed using empirically tested methods, and represent the analysis of thousands of cases over years of performance, it would be wise to override them only when you know something the scorecard does not. These situations include:

- Company policy rules, as discussed earlier.
- Local knowledge. For example, the branch staff in banks may know the applicant and the local environment and be able to use

information such as family income, recent job history, local economy, and so forth to make a better decision. This can be both positive information and negative.

- Justifiable derogatory performance. For example, a person was unemployed and missed payments but now has a well-paying job, or a student missed payments on a small debt during vacations.
- Due diligence and paperwork. For example, not being able to furnish satisfactory mortgage/car loan papers or income confirmation.
- Other exceptional circumstances where the predicted risk level using a scorecard alone is not representative.

Overriding levels vary depending on the product and amount of human intervention allowed in credit processing. Typically, low-value/high-volume products where automated decision making (i.e., a sole arbiter situation) is used, such as credit cards, have very low override rates. However, high-value products such as business loans and mortgages, which are processed manually and require more due diligence to be performed, have higher override rates. Override rates are also higher in environments where the scorecard is used as a decision support tool, that is, as one of many items looked at, rather than the sole basis for decision making. In addition, in cases where scorecards are developed with too few characteristics (instead of a broad based "risk profile" scorecard), overriding tends to be high. This is generally because the scorecard only captures a few items, and therefore much more information is left outside of the scorecard for overriding, and because such narrow-based scorecards generate less confidence among adjudicators, leading to higher second guessing of the scorecard.

In either case, lowside overriding should be kept to a minimum— and where it is allowed, performance must be monitored, preferably by "override reason code" where available. Furthermore, every attempt should be made not to allow a "miscellaneous" attribute in the override reason code, because this can become a proxy for judgmental overrides, as opposed to overrides due to more legitimate factors on both the high side and the low side. This is to ensure that overriding done on the basis of experience (or lack thereof) and "gut feel" is validated through performance, and curbed where necessary. Regulators tend to want overrides to be in the 3%–5% range, at most, in a scoring environment. It is important to monitor specific reasons for overrides and monitor trends. In mortgage lending, higher override rates for applicants falling into protected classes are a definite red flag.

CHAPTER 9

Scorecard Development Process, Stage 7: Postimplementation

There are two main areas of postimplementation works:

1. Reporting
2. Review

SCORECARD AND PORTFOLIO MONITORING REPORTS

This section deals with some of the standard reports used by risk practitioners to monitor scorecard and portfolio performance. Most scorecard and portfolio management reports that are produced are associated with portfolio and scorecard performance statistics, such as approval rates, bad rates, override rates, and various indices. There are, however, some important business reasons and goals for which these reports should be run. These goals, and the reports used to meet them, are detailed below.

Scorecard and application management reports:

- Confirm "the future is like the past." Scorecards are developed with a certain applicant or customer profile in mind (represented by score or characteristic distribution). This assumption needs to be validated on an ongoing basis.

- System stability (also called population stability and scorecard stability) report
- Scorecard characteristic analysis
- Nonscorecard characteristic analysis

- Monitor and pinpoint sources of change in the profiles of applicants and approves (or customers for behavior scoring). Just knowing that a change has taken place is insufficient, as it does not lead to any actionable items. The source of (and reasons for) the change must also be identified.
  - Scorecard and nonscorecard characteristic analysis
  - Analysis of competition and marketing campaigns
  - Analysis by region and other segments
- Track risk profile of incoming customers and applicants.
  - System stability report
  - Scorecard and nonscorecard characteristic analysis
  - Score distribution of approves/customers report
- Generate statistics for acceptance/override.
  - Final score report
  - Override report

For portfolio management reports:

- Monitor risk performance of accounts.
  - Delinquency report
  - Vintage analysis
  - Delinquency migration report
  - Roll rate across time report
- Monitor and pinpoint the sources of delinquency and profit. As discussed previously, knowing where your losses are coming from allows you to take risk-adjusted decisions.
  - Delinquency report, by region and other segments
  - Marketing campaign and competitive analysis
- Estimate future loss rates.
  - Vintage analysis and roll rate report
- Evaluate bad rate predictions and manage expectations. Tracking

actual performance against expected allows for adjustments for future loss forecasts.
- Vintage analysis
- Delinquency report
- Delinquency migration report

The preceding applies to both application and behavior scorecard reports.

Needless to say, proper reporting and tracking structures must be in place prior to implementation, so that early results of new scorecard or strategy implementation can be tracked. At the initial stages of scorecard implementation in production environments, it is recommended that weekly reports be produced so that any deviations from expected performance can be identified quickly and remedied. When it is determined that the scorecards or strategies are performing as expected, regular monthly or quarterly reporting is sufficient.

While the credit business is dynamic, its pace is fairly slow. Unlike market risk, where fluctuations in risk factors can occur by the minute, retail credit risk indicators and factors tend to change over a larger time frame. It is therefore important to identify trends, not quirks, especially when a decision needs to be changed. In the "Preimplementation Validation" section in Chapter 8, it was recommended that System Stability reports be run on applicants from the last three and six months; the reasoning was to catch long-term trends before deciding whether the scorecard was still valid or not. The reasoning here is no different—whether trying to decide if the scorecard is still valid, or to determine if a cutoff for a particular segment needs to be changed, or to institute harsher delinquency or credit authorization treatment for a particular cohort or segment, you need to be sure that the results are indicative of a long-term continuing trend rather than a one-off event.

Finally, as was emphasized in the chapters on scorecard development, the business reasons for changes in profiles and performances must be explained. It is not enough merely to look at approval statistics, bad rates, or stability indices—to be able to make informed/risk-adjusted decisions, you must be able to explain why things are happening.

Scorecard Management Reports

These reports are often called "front-end" reports because they are used to track incoming applications.

System/Population/Scorecard Stability Report   This report has been covered previously (in Chapter 8) for preimplementation validation. During preimplementation validation, the score distributions of the latest batch of applicants were compared with those of the development sample to measure any differences. The objective and method here are exactly the same. This report also compares the distributions by score of the current applicant population ("actual") with those of the development sample ("expected"). This is done to detect shifts in the applicant profile, represented by the distribution of applications by score. The report can easily be modified for behavioral scoring by comparing distributions of existing customers with the distributions by score of the development sample. This comparison provides two pieces of information:

1. It validates the "the future is reflected by the past" assumption (i.e., bad rate predictions are based on a future applicant profile that is similar to the one used for predictive modeling). While not conclusive, evidence of similarity provides a comfort level.

2. It provides an indication of the quality of applicants/accounts (e.g., if the shifts in scores are downward, that may point to a deteriorating quality of applicant pool, or existing customers).

System stability reports are generally produced monthly; however, quarterly reporting may be sufficient for stable portfolios. A point to note is that for a pure system stability report, the applicant population must be generated using the same exclusion criteria as the development sample. Companies that choose to score exclusions, however, perform a second set of analyses for the scorecard cutoff, in which all applicants are included. This is to provide a more realistic analysis of the expected approval rate, and of the effects of the cutoff on key segments.

An example of a system stability report is shown in Exhibit 9.1. Note that the system stability report is also sometimes referred to as the population stability or scorecard stability report.

The "Actual %" and "Expected %" columns denote the distribution of cases for recent and development samples, respectively, for each of the score ranges specified. Note that in the exhibit, the scores have been grouped such that each score bucket contains 10% of the "expected" population. This has been done for efficiency, so that any shifts upward or downward can easily be identified (by setting the base for each group to 10%).

There are two types of analyses that can be done with Exhibit 9.1. First, the nature of the population shift can be confirmed by viewing a graph of the actual versus expected applicant/account distributions by score. This can provide additional information (e.g., whether the shift in scores is downward, upward, or kurtosis). In addition, displaying the distributions for historical periods in addition to the most recent month or quarter—for example, for the last three months, last six months, and so forth—on the same graph will help in tracking long-term trends. This will indicate whether, for example, there is slowly deteriorating quality or whether the distribution tends to follow cyclical variations. A change that is a long-term trend can be taken as a stable event and therefore reacted to with policy changes and other decisions. This is a better way to guide decision making, as opposed to reacting to monthly variations that are not stable.

EXHIBIT 9.1   SYSTEM STABILITY REPORT

Score Range	Actual %	Expected %	(A-E)	A/E	ln(A/E)	Index
0–169	7%	10%	−3%	0.7000	−0.3567	0.0107
170–179	6%	10%	−4%	0.6000	−0.5108	0.0204
180–189	6%	10%	−4%	0.6000	−0.5108	0.0204
190–199	7%	10%	−3%	0.7000	−0.3567	0.0107
200–209	9%	10%	−1%	0.9000	−0.1054	0.0011
210–219	13%	10%	3%	1.3000	0.2624	0.0079
220–229	13%	10%	3%	1.3000	0.2624	0.0079
230–239	11%	10%	1%	1.1000	0.0953	0.0010
240–249	13%	10%	3%	1.3000	0.2624	0.0079
250+	15%	10%	5%	1.5000	0.4055	0.0203
Index						**0.1081**

Exhibit 9.2 compares the distributions of expected, most current actual, actual from last three months, and actual from last six months on the same graph. The numbers for current actual and expected have been taken from Exhibit 9.1. Exhibit 9.2 clearly shows that the applicants have been consistently scoring higher and higher for the last six months.

Second, the actual magnitude of the shift can be measured mathematically. This is nothing more than measuring the difference between two distributions. One method of doing this is by using an industry standard measure, as shown in Exhibit 8.7. The index as shown measures the magnitude of the population shift between recent applicants and expected (from development sample). This index is calculated as:

$$\sum (\% \text{ Actual} - \% \text{ Expected}) \times ln\ (\% \text{ Actual} / \% \text{ Expected})$$

for all score ranges.

This calculation is exactly like that for Information Value, seen earlier in Chapter 6; it measures the deviation between two distributions.

In general, the index can be interpreted as follows:

- Less than 0.10 shows no significant change.
- 0.10–0.25 shows a small change that needs to be investigated.

EXHIBIT 9.2   **SYSTEM STABILITY TREND**

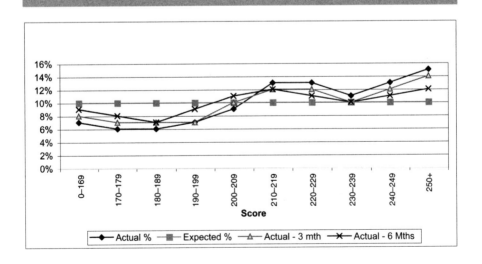

- Greater than 0.25 points to a significant shift in the applicant population.

Other methods, such as Chi Square with some level of significance, may also be used to measure the magnitude of the shift. The method shown here is one used widely by credit risk managers.

This index is not an end-all measure; it only provides a general indication. In fact, it only tells us whether a shift has occurred or not, and provides an indication of the magnitude of the shift. Factors such as trends (Is the change a temporary occurrence or something more long-term?), magnitude of the shift, and reasons for change should be taken into account before deciding if a population shift is significant. From the perspective of being able to use this report to generate decisions, the more important task here is to find out the reasons for the shifts in scores.

Shifts in scores can be due to several reasons:

- Independent change in applicant profile (e.g., demographic change).
- Market dynamics that include things such as marketing campaigns, niche competition, and product design. For example, if the recent month's applicants were noticeably younger or were concentrated in a particular area, this may be due to focused marketing activity. Changes in product design such as the addition of loyalty programs, changes in fee structure, "no interest for six months"–type sweeteners, or shift to nontraditional channels can also attract a different type of applicant. External competition attracting a particular demographic may also affect the makeup of your applicants. Examples include institutions that target customers through product design (e.g., Telco's using advertising and handsets to attract young customers), loyalty programs, and higher interest rates. One bank that did not have a loyalty program associated with its credit card found that its applicant quality became consistently worse over time—analysis showed that most of its applicants were those who were rejected by banks that offered loyalty programs with their credit card (i.e., those who could, got credit cards that offered

fringe benefits, while those who could not went to this particular bank). In behavior scoring, more aggressive authorizations or credit line management strategies, introduction of loyalty programs, repricing, cross-selling, and other such activities can change the score profile of existing customers.

- Error in coding. This is typically a systematic error.
- Mistakes in data capture, whereby the data represents a nonrandom or incorrectly segmented sample, or where exclusions from the development sample are included.

There are several ways to perform further investigation to pinpoint the cause of the shift. These include:

- Performing a scorecard characteristic analysis to analyze shifts in characteristics in the scorecard. (This may sound obvious, but this is done because the scores are based on the scorecard. Again, this underscores the importance of building a widely based "risk profile" scorecard so that shifts indicated in these analyses reflect reality and are not just caused by fluctuations in one or two characteristics of a narrowly based scorecard.)
- Analyzing shifts in nonscorecard characteristics. These fall into three main categories:
  - Strong characteristics that did not enter the scorecard. (Since these are risk rankers, their distributions should confirm qualitatively if the population is getting better or worse.)
  - Characteristics related to those that are in the scorecard. (These should move in the same direction as those in the scorecard, thus providing confirmation for shifts in the scorecard characteristics.)
  - Numerators and denominators for ratios in scorecard.
- Gathering information on changes in regulations, recent marketing campaigns internally and by the competition, and product changes for both.

Scorecard Characteristic Analysis Report   The scorecard characteristic analysis report compares current versus development distributions for each scorecard characteristic, and the impact on the score of any distribution shifts. This report can further pinpoint the reasons for any shifts in scores, and is generally produced quarterly, or whenever the system stability report indicates a significant shift. As with the system stability report, it is again advisable to compare expected distributions with those from the most recent period as well as historical periods, to detect trends.

An example of a scorecard characteristic analysis for "Age" is shown in Exhibit 9.3.

"Expected %" and "Actual %" again refer to the distributions of the development and recent samples, respectively. There are two analyses that can be performed with this data. First, the expected and current, as well as historical, distributions for each characteristic can be plotted on a chart, like the one shown in Exhibit 9.2. That will provide a visual indication of the nature of the shift.

Second, we can calculate the magnitude of that shift mathematically. In this case, we will calculate the impact of that shift in terms of scores. This impact, or the scorecard characteristic index, is calculated simply by:

$$\sum (\% \text{ Actual} - \% \text{ Expected}) \times (\text{Points})$$

for all score ranges.

Note that including a "% Accept by criteria" column in this analysis can provide indication of whether the scorecard is systematically discriminating against a particular segment.

Exhibit 9.3 shows a shift toward a younger applicant, resulting in applicants scoring about 2.63 points less than expected for age.

EXHIBIT 9.3   SCORECARD CHARACTERISTIC ANALYSIS

Age	Expected %	Actual %	Points	Index
18–24	12%	21%	10	0.9
25–29	19%	25%	15	0.9
30–37	32%	28%	25	−1
38–45	12%	6%	28	−1.68
46+	25%	20%	35	−1.75
Index				**−2.63**

Similar reports are produced for all the characteristics in the score-card, and usually placed on one page to be analyzed. An example of this (from a partial application scorecard) is shown in Exhibit 9.4.

Analyzing the characteristics shown above, one can conclude:

- Applicants are getting younger (therefore riskier).
- They are living at their residences less (riskier). Other time-related characteristics outside of the scorecard should also point in the same direction.
- They have not moved geographically.
- They have a significantly higher number of inquiries at the credit bureau in the last six months (riskier). Analysis of inquiries in the last three months and last twelve months will confirm whether this is a short-term phenomenon or something more permanent.

EXHIBIT 9.4   FULL SCORECARD CHARACTERISTIC ANALYSIS

Age	Expected	Actual	Points	Index	# Delq	Expected	Actual	Points	Index
18–24	12%	21%	10	0.9	0	80%	65%	45	−6.75
25–29	19%	25%	15	0.9	1–2	12%	21%	20	1.8
30–37	32%	28%	25	−1	3–5	5%	8%	12	0.36
38–45	12%	6%	28	−1.68	6+	3%	6%	5	0.15
46+	25%	20%	35	−1.75					**−4.44**
				−2.63	**Utilization at Bureau**				
Time at Res					0	12%	8%	15	−0.6
0–6	18%	29%	12	1.32	1–9	10%	19%	40	3.6
7–18	32%	32%	25	0	10–25	14%	20%	30	1.8
19–36	26%	22%	28	−1.12	26–50	22%	25%	25	0.75
37+	24%	17%	40	−2.8	50–69	11%	6%	20	−1
				−2.6	70–85	13%	9%	15	−0.6
Region					86–99	14%	8%	10	−0.6
Major Urban	55%	58%	20	0.6	100+	4%	5%	5	0.05
Minor Urban	26%	24%	25	−0.5					**3.4**
Rural	19%	18%	15	−0.15					
				−0.05					
Inq 6 mth									
0	63%	34%	40	−11.6					
1–3	19%	31%	30	3.6					
4–5	10%	16%	15	0.9					
6+	8%	19%	10	1.1					
				−6					

- The number of delinquencies from bureau data is higher (riskier). Other bureau delinquency related characteristics should confirm this.
- Utilization of revolving credit from bureau data is lower (less risky).

While all other indicators point to a higher-risk pool of applicants, the utilization levels indicate otherwise. Trends like this are counterintuitive and should be investigated. In this case, the balances and credit lines (i.e., the numerator and denominator for calculating utilization) were tracked separately. While average balances showed slight increases from historical levels, the credit lines had increased by a higher amount. This had happened in a highly competitive environment where banks had increased the credit lines of customers to be more competitive— obviously without taking into account the increased riskiness of their clients. Therefore applicants were scoring higher for utilization, but this did not represent lower risk.

This underscores the need to add business reasoning to score analyses, beyond simply calculating score shifts.

In cases such as these, where the Risk Manager is aware that applicants are scoring higher than they should, some options that can be considered are:

- Reduce points assigned for utilization, for higher-risk applicants.
- Increase the cutoff.
- Adjust expected loss/bad rates to reflect a higher actual risk than what is indicated by scores.

The preceding analysis is therefore enhanced from a simple calculation of score shifts to something resembling a key risk indicator (KRI)– type analysis for applicants (or customers, for behavior scorecards).

A natural extension of this analysis is to compare development and current distributions for other characteristics outside of the scorecard. These can include:

- Characteristics that are not in the scorecard, but are believed to have an impact on applicant quality. These include strong characteristics that did not make it into the scorecard. For example, if shifts in the scorecard characteristics point to a deteriorating quality of applicants, reviewing these strong nonscorecard characteristics will help to confirm that movement. This ensures that judgments on applicant quality are made with a wider variety of information and therefore more robust.

- Characteristics that are similar to the ones in the scorecard. For example, if "age" is in the scorecard, tracking other time-related characteristics—such as time at employment or address, and age of oldest trade—may explain further reasons for the shift in applicant profile. If "inquiries in the last 6 months" is in the scorecard, tracking inquiries in the last 3 and 12 months will help to further explain the shift in inquiries. In the example in Exhibit 9.4, the distribution for "inquiries in the last 12 months" did not show any significant change. This meant that the increase in inquiries may be due to increasing competition in the last six months, or it may mean that factors such as product change or marketing in the last six months may be attracting a more credit-hungry applicant. Related characteristics should all move in the same direction (e.g., older applicants should have higher tenures at work or older files at the bureau). Examples of other information types for which this can be done include trades, demographics, inquiries, and financial ratios.

- Where ratios are used in the scorecard, distributions of the denominator and numerator should also be tracked to explain changes in the ratio itself. For example, if utilization (balance divided by credit limit) has decreased, it may be due to either balances moving lower or credit limits being increased (as shown in Exhibit 9.4).

Again, these analyses should be performed to compare development data with recent historical data over the last one to six months to detect any trends, and to validate that the shifts in distributions are not a temporary phenomenon.

The shifts in scored and nonscored characteristics should be consistent and explainable using logic and business considerations. If, for example, analysis shows that applicants are getting younger, yet have higher "time at employment," coding errors may be occurring. Such illogical shifts must be investigated and explained.

Final Score Report   The final score report is used for application scorecards, and is produced to obtain operational numbers such as approval rate and override rate. It can also be used to monitor excessive overriding and gauge the quality of applicants and approved accounts. Exhibit 9.5 shows a typical final score report, using a scorecard with a cutoff of 200 points.

This exhibit shows an approval rate of 64.2%, and lowside and highside override rates of 4.84% and 9.09%, respectively. Note that some lenders calculate override rates based on the total applicants as the denominator, while others use the number of applicants below or above cutoff as the denominator (for lowside and highside override).

For products such as mortgages and loans, an additional "Not Taken Up" column is also created to denote those who were approved by the lender but chose not to accept the offer. In scorecard development, these are considered indeterminate.

The report in Exhibit 9.5 is typically produced for each scorecard, but many users will also generate it for various subpopulations and segments. This is done to ensure that a valuable segment is not being penal-

EXHIBIT 9.5   FINAL SCORE REPORT

Score Range	Applicants	Approved	% Approved	Lowside	Highside
0–169	700	—	0%	0	
170–179	800	16	2%	16	
180–189	700	35	5%	35	
190–199	900	99	11%	99	
200–209	1,100	924	84%		176
210–219	1,100	968	88%		132
220–229	1,000	900	90%		100
230–239	1,200	1,092	91%		108
240–249	1,100	1,045	95%		55
250+	1,400	1,344	96%		56
	10,000	6,423	**64.2%**	150	627
Above Cutoff	6,900	6,273		**4.84%**	**9.09%**
Below Cutoff	3,100	150			

ized, or that approval rate by score is consistent across various segments. Evidence indicating that this is not happening may mean that the scorecard is either not predicting as designed, or that excessive overriding is going on. In the first case, alternate segmentation may be required, whereas in the second, further investigation and controls would be called for.

A variation of Exhibit 9.5 is one that tracks the quality of booked business across time. An example is shown in Exhibit 9.6.

This exhibit shows the distribution of booked accounts by score, over three time periods. These are compared to the expected distribution to determine if the quality of accounts is worse or better than what was expected. Exhibit 9.6 shows a constant decline in quality, where the proportion of approves in the 200–209 score band (just above cutoff) is increasing, while those in the top score band are decreasing. In addition, not only is the percentage of lowside overrides gradually increasing, but they are being done at increasingly lower scores.

While the System Stability and Final Score reports show quality of applicants, this report indicates the quality of approved accounts. This report helps to generate a better expected bad rate of each new intake of accounts, instead of relying on a simple approval rate/bad rate relationship derived from the gains tables. That relationship—which tells you that if your approval rate is, for example, 70%, then you can expect a total bad rate of 3%—is based on the assumption that the distribution of accounts above cutoff remains stable. As shown in Exhibit 9.6, once

| EXHIBIT 9.6 | ACCOUNT QUALITY |

Score	Expected	Q1 03	Q2 03	Q3 03	Q4 03
0–169	0%	0%	1%	1%	
170–179	0%	1%	3%	4%	
180–189	0%	2%	3%	5%	
190–199	0%	2%	4%	5%	
200–209	20%	26%	28%	26%	
210–219	15%	19%	20%	20%	
220–229	20%	22%	22%	20%	
230–239	16%	15%	12%	11%	
240–249	18%	4%	3%	5%	
250+	11%	9%	4%	3%	
Total	100%	100%	100%	100%	

that assumption is no longer valid, one must reevaluate the bad rate predictions. In some cases, the approval rate can stay the same for a given
portfolio, but if the mix changes, then the predictions from the gains
tables are no longer valid.

Override Report   This report tracks the number of lowside and highside overrides by override reason code. In situations where decisions are
made both manually and automatically (i.e., by software), the overrides
need to be tracked by both those decision types as well.

As discussed in the "Overrides" section of Chapter 8, excessive and
uncontrolled overriding results in increased losses, yet some overriding is
justified and should be done. This report therefore acts as a control tool
to alert management when override levels increase, or when overriding
is done for unspecified reasons. It can also be used to determine the quality of overrides being done within the organization. Where possible, all
overriding should be done based on justifiable and trackable reasons, so
that analysis can be done to determine which override reasons are appropriate and which ones should be abandoned. One way of determining
this is to generate a report of performance by override reason.

A sample override report is shown in Exhibit 9.7.

This exhibit shows overrides by reason and decision type. Note that
the definitions of system and manual decisions will vary across compa-

EXHIBIT 9.7   OVERRIDE REPORT

Override Reason	Number	System 'D'	System 'A'	Manual 'D'	Manual 'A'
Lowside					
Local Knowledge	34	34	0		34
Justifiable Delq	96	96	0		96
VIP	12	12	0		12
VP Override	8	8	0		8
	150	150	0		150
Highside					
Bankruptcy	125	120	0		5
Local Knowledge	102	0	102	102	
Derogatory	200	0	200	185	15
Policy 1	55	55	0		
Policy 2	73	73	0		
Policy 3	92	92	0		
	647	340	302	287	20

nies, depending on their approval process. Some organizations require an adjudicator to review and confirm system decisions for all applications, while others automatically approve or decline the majority of applications with few manual reviews. The report shown in Exhibit 9.7 can therefore be customized to include "Preliminary Decision" and "Final Decision" instead of system and manual decisions.

Note also that this report does not include "Other" or "None Specified" as reason codes. These should, of course, be minimized. A good practice before designing application processing systems and reports is to survey adjudicators, to compile a comprehensive list of all reasons they have used to override applications. These reasons can then be subdivided into groups. This practice minimizes the chances of overrides based on reasons that cannot be entered into a system.

For lowside overrides, all decisions are shown as "System 'D'" and "Manual 'A,'" meaning that the system declined all of them (for scoring below cutoff), but they were all finally approved by someone, based on a specified reason.

The highside override portion has a few variations:

- "Bankruptcy" shows that all 125 overrides were declined by the system, indicating that presence of bankruptcy is an automated policy decline. However, five people were ultimately approved by an adjudicator, despite having previous bankruptcy.

- Policy rules 1, 2, and 3 are also examples of automated policy declines.

- "Local Knowledge" shows all 102 applicants being approved by the system, and then being subsequently declined manually by someone, possibly at the branch level.

- "Derogatory" (i.e., delinquent performance at the bureau or in-house) shows an interesting situation. All 200 applicants were initially approved by the system—meaning that the particular derogatory performance is not an automated policy rule. Subsequently, while 185 of them were manually declined due to the derogatory information, the adjudicator decided to approve 15.

The setup shown in Exhibit 9.7 can therefore be used to monitor overrides better than a simple distribution by override reason, which can sometime mask certain sorts of decisions, such as the highside override manual approves for bankruptcy shown. If a report is generated based on the logic of "if score > cutoff and decision = approve" to define approved accounts, it will fail to recognize the five bankrupts as overrides and include them as normal approves. One can also argue that the 15 applicants with some derogatory information that were manually discovered and approved are also overrides. In such cases, these should be tracked separately to gauge the effectiveness of the decision to approve accounts with that derogatory information.

In environments where the override rate is high, an additional report should be done, outlining the risk profile of the overrides. This can be done in various ways, for example:

- Compare scorecard and nonscorecard characteristics for overrides and nonoverrides, especially for negative performance characteristics such as "Worst Delinquency."
- Score distribution of overrides across time.

This is to enable a qualitative assessment of the risk profile of those being overridden.

Portfolio Performance Reports

Portfolio performance reports are often called "back-end" reports. They involve analyzing the delinquency performance of accounts

Delinquency (or Performance) Report   Delinquency (or performance) reports are used to determine the performance of the portfolio. These typically consist of charts displaying bad rates by score for different definitions of bad. In addition, this report is also generated for various segments (e.g., region, channel, demographics, etc.) to identify particular areas of high or low delinquencies. This report is also produced for accounts by "month opened" to identify any specific cohorts that present a higher risk.

An example of a Delinquency report by account for a credit card portfolio is shown in Exhibit 9.8.

This report can be generated for both counts (as shown in Exhibit 9.8) or dollars receivable, and is applicable to both behavior and application scoring. Exhibit 9.8 shows:

- Performance by an application scorecard with a cutoff at 200.

- A separate column for active accounts (i.e., those who have utilized their available credit). The definition of "active" differs between lenders but is typically based on recency of usage.

- "Bad rate" for each delinquency level, using the total number of active accounts as the denominator. Some lenders use the total number of opened accounts as the base for revolving portfolios. For products such as mortgages and loans, the total accounts opened or actively paying should be used as the denominator. If the scorecard was developed based on a complex bad definition such as "1 × 90 days or 2 × 60 days or 3 × 30 days," then a column needs to be added with that definition so that the actual performance of the scorecard can be evaluated. Note that if behavior scorecards were being developed, this report would provide an indication of the approximate number of bads that may be available for development.

- A trend of increasing bad rate as the score decreases, as should be the case. This shows that the scorecard is risk ranking.

The definition of "bad" here can be based on either "ever" bad or "currently" bad; some lenders do produce reports based on both these definitions.

In some cases, the performance of accounts just below cutoff (low-side overrides) is better than those just above cutoff. This is mainly due to "cherry-picking" (i.e., those below cutoff were manually selected after careful review as "best of the bunch," while those above cutoff were automatically approved).

This report is based on delinquency performance—similar reports can be generated for churn, profit, revenue, recovery, or any other objective for which the scorecard was developed.

EXHIBIT 9.8   DELINQUENCY PERFORMANCE REPORT

Score	Accounts	Active	%	Current	%	1-29 days	%	30-59	%	60-89	%	90+	%	Writeoff	%	Bankrupt	%
0-169	200	198	99%	127	64%	22	10.9%	15	7.50%	12	6.10%	9	4.50%	6	3.00%	8	4.00%
170-179	348	300	86%	207	69%	36	12.0%	20	6.80%	9	3.00%	9	3.10%	9	3.10%	9	3.00%
180-189	435	367	84%	264	72%	48	13.0%	15	4.00%	12	3.20%	10	2.80%	8	2.20%	10	2.80%
190-199	466	387	83%	286	74%	43	11.0%	21	5.50%	11	2.80%	8	1.94%	10	2.56%	9	2.20%
200-209	2,456	1,876	76%	1,482	79%	225	12.0%	43	2.30%	47	2.48%	18	0.96%	39	2.10%	22	1.16%
210-219	4,563	3,600	79%	2,952	82%	342	9.5%	93	2.58%	83	2.30%	23	0.65%	67	1.87%	40	1.10%
220-229	5,678	4,325	76%	3,676	85%	389	9.0%	93	2.16%	67	1.54%	14	0.32%	51	1.18%	35	0.80%
230-239	7,658	4,598	60%	4,046	88%	359	7.8%	87	1.90%	41	0.90%	18	0.40%	28	0.60%	18	0.40%
240-249	5,786	3,546	61%	3,333	94%	142	4.0%	35	1.00%	18	0.50%	—	0.00%	7	0.20%	11	0.30%
250+	4,987	2,176	44%	2,089	96%	44	2.0%	17	0.80%	9	0.40%	9	0.40%	4	0.20%	4	0.20%
Total	32,577	21,373	66%	18,463	86%	1,648	7.71%	441	2.06%	307	1.44%	118	0.55%	230	1.08%	165	0.77%

Another object of performance monitoring is to evaluate the accuracy of the scorecard. For a proper comparison, the actual account performance should be based on the same criteria as the scorecard development sample (i.e., with the same "bad" definition, segmentation, performance window, and exclusions). An example of such a comparison is shown in Exhibit 9.9.

This exhibit shows the actual bad rate of a portfolio (Bad %) compared to that expected at development (Exp Bad %). There are several factors to note here:

- Since this report cannot be generated until the performance window has been reached, it has limited operational value. In most cases, vintage analysis and charts like the one shown in Exhibit 4.3 are used to track the performance of individual cohorts against that expected. If a cohort has better performance, it can be concluded that the expected bad rate at maturity would be less than expected, and vice versa. This information is useful for managing accounts and for forecasting.

- Actual performance is almost always different from expected, due to account management strategies. What is important to the Risk Manager is to be able to accurately predict the expected performance at any given time.

EXHIBIT 9.9   SCORECARD ACCURACY

Score	Accounts	Active	%	Bad	%	Exp Bad %
0–169	200	198	99%	35	18%	23.0%
170–179	348	300	86%	37	12%	18.0%
180–189	435	367	84%	40	11%	14.0%
190–199	466	387	83%	37	10%	10.0%
200–209	2,456	1,876	76%	126	7%	8.0%
210–219	4,563	3,600	79%	213	6%	5.0%
220–229	5,678	4,325	76%	166	4%	4.0%
230–239	7,658	4,598	60%	106	2%	2.0%
240–249	5,786	3,546	61%	35	1%	0.8%
250+	4,987	2,176	44%	26	1%	0.5%
Total	32,577	21,373	66%	821	4%	

- The ongoing monitoring of bad rates by time opened, and comparisons to expected performance are used to evaluate whether or not the scorecard is indeed working. In most cases, scorecards do rank risk, but the predicted bad rates are not as expected. Where the scorecard does not rank risk, it may need to be replaced. In cases where there is disparity between expected and predicted performance, actions such as changing cutoffs (for some segments if applicable), changing policy rules, or reweighting the scores may be necessary.

Vintage (or Cohort) Analysis   Vintage, or cohort, analysis involves generating the bad rates for different cohorts (accounts opened within a particular time frame) by time on books.

As with the delinquency report, this report is also produced for different definitions of bad, and for various segments and subpopulations. The report is used to:

- Identify high-risk cohorts (i.e., if accounts opened in a particular month or quarter are a higher-risk than others).
- Tracks bad rate development over time—note that Exhibit 4.3, which shows the development of bad rate over time, was developed using information from a cohort analysis table shown in Exhibit 4.2. This information is used to compare the performance of new cohorts to long-term performance, in order to manage expectations and produce more accurate forecasts.

An example of a vintage analysis is shown in Exhibit 9.10. It shows the performance of accounts opened from January 2003 to March 2004, measured after equivalent tenures as accounts (in this case, based on quarters). Note that similar reports can be generated for other metrics such as churn, profit, bankruptcy, recovery, and so forth, based on business objectives as well as the target specified for scorecard development.

This report can be run for different definitions of bad (e.g., ever 90 days, ever 60 days, and so forth). Exhibit 9.10 shows that accounts opened in March and April 2003 are of a higher risk than those opened

EXHIBIT 9.10 VINTAGE ANALYSIS

Open Date	1 Qtr	2 Qtr	3 Qtr	4 Qtr	5 Qtr
Jan–03	0.00%	0.44%	0.87%	1.40%	2.40%
Feb–03	0.00%	0.37%	0.88%	1.70%	2.30%
Mar–03	0.00%	0.42%	0.92%	**1.86%**	**2.80%**
Apr–03	0.00%	**0.65%**	**1.20%**	**1.90%**	
May–03	0.00%	0.10%	0.80%	1.20%	
Jun–03	0.00%	0.14%	0.79%	1.50%	
Jul–03	0.00%	0.23%	0.88%		
Aug–03	0.00%	0.16%	0.73%		
Sep–03	0.00%	0.13%	0.64%		
Oct–03	0.20%	**0.54%**			
Nov–03	0.00%	**0.46%**			
Dec–03	0.00%	0.38%			
Jan–04	0.00%				
Feb–04	0.00%				
Mar–04	0.00%				

in other months. At this point, one can refer to system stability and other reports from March and April 2003 to find out reasons for this disparity in performance. It may be due to factors such as adverse selection, changes in cutoff, marketing efforts targeted to high-risk groups, system errors whereby high-risk customers were inadvertently approved, or excessive overriding. In short, one needs to be able to use nearly all the reports covered in this chapter as well as information on historical business practices to get these reasons.

Once those reasons are known, it can be determined if they represent a one-off event, or if the conditions are in place to cause a repeat. In the case of the latter, steps can be taken to avoid approving such high-risk accounts.

In addition, once it is discovered that particular cohorts are of a higher risk compared to others in their peer groups, risk-adjusted decisions can be made to control them. These include:

- Increasing pricing for loan renewals
- Curbing automated credit line increases by flagging high-risk cohorts so that their credit limits are only increased on demand and after review

- Curbing credit card customers from using their cards during delinquency or from going over their assigned credit limit
- Introducing more stringent collections actions for these cohorts

Using information from reports to drive this kind of decision making is key. It makes the report a decision-making tool, and not just an exercise in generating paperwork and statistics.

The sort of research into the past mentioned previously (to understand the reasons for disparity in cohort performance) is made easier if certain items are documented. These include:

- Changes in scorecards, cutoffs, policy rules, products, and regulatory environment
- Information on major marketing initiatives

These should be captured for each portfolio, and documented such that future diagnosis and troubleshooting is made easier. Such documentation is common in credit scoring, and is often referred to as the Portfolio Chronology Log. Note that this is separate from the Data Change Log, which captures all changes to databases within the organization.

Delinquency Migration Report   On a month-to-month basis, most lenders track the movement of accounts from one delinquency bucket to another. An example of such a delinquency migration report is provided in Exhibit 9.11.

The report shown in Exhibit 9.11 measures the migration of number of accounts from one delinquency class to another, from "previous month" to "this month." Note that the "%" measure in the "Previous Month" column is a column-wise distribution. The "%" fields under "This Month" are a row-wise distribution. For example, of all accounts that were 30–59 days past due last month, 40% are now current, 10% are 1–29 days past due, 14.5% are 30–59 days past due, and so forth. The same report is also produced for dollars in each delinquency bucket.

Reports such as these can help in forecasting. This one can be modified to provide long-term roll rates over many years. In some cases,

EXHIBIT 9.11   DELINQUENCY MIGRATION

Previous Month	Previous Month		This Month															
	#	%	Current		1–29 days		30–59 days		60–89 days		90–119 days		120–179 days		180+		Bankrupt	
			#	%	#	%	#	%	#	%	#	%	#	%	#	%	#	%
Current	54,782	72%	52,591	96.0%	2,082	3.8%											210	0.2%
1–29 days	12,640	17%	10,112	80.0%	632	5.0%	1,871	14.8%									85	0.2%
30–59 days	3,254	4%	1,302	40.0%	325	10.0%	472	14.5%	1,139	35.0%							59	0.5%
60–89 days	2,271	3%	182	8.0%	204	9.0%	227	10.0%	227	10.0%	1,413	62.2%					39	0.8%
90–119 days	1,449	2%	55	3.8%	65	4.5%	80	5.5%	87	6.0%	72	5.0%	1,065	73.1%			42	2.1%
120–179	887	1.2%	16	1.8%	12	1.4%	19	2.1%	20	2.2%	27	3.0%	64	4.0%	550	78.0%	150	7.5%
180+	632	0.8%	1	0.2%	8	1.2%	11	1.8%	16	2.5%	13	2.0%	3	3.0%	371	60.3%	210	29.0%
Total	75,915		64,258	85%	3,329	4%	2,679	3.5%	1,488	2.0%	1,524	2.0%	1,132	1.5%	921	1.2%	585	0.8%

where the development of 90-day or chargeoff models is not possible, models to predict lesser delinquency, e.g., 60 days, can be developed. The forecast from the model can then be combined with roll rate information to then predict 90-day delinquency or chargeoff. The report is similar to the roll rate analysis discussed in Chapter 4, and provides similar evidence of "point of no return" for delinquency. The report above shows that 80% of those who were 1–29 days past due last month paid up to become current, while only 2% of those who were 90–119 days past due paid up fully.

Roll Rate across Time   A modification of Exhibit 9.11 tracks the number of accounts and dollars outstanding in each delinquency bucket across time. An example of such a report is shown in Exhibit 9.12, which only shows two delinquency buckets, for illustration purposes. In reality, it would be produced for all delinquency buckets.

This report helps you to understand the development of delinquency across time, in terms of both accounts that are delinquent and dollars. The relative growth of dollars delinquent to account also gives an indication of rising balances and whether the loss given default is rising or not.

EXHIBIT 9.12   ROLL RATE

Month	Total Receivable		Current				1–29 days			
	Accounts	Dollars	Accounts	%	Dollars	%	Accounts	%	Dollars	%
May-04	80,895	$256,987	71,188	88.0%	$230,260	89.6%	$6,472	8.0%	$35,978	14.0%
Jun-04	81,229	$277,125	71,075	87.5%	$245,533	88.6%	$6,986	8.6%	$36,026	13.0%
Jul-04	86,985	$289,541	75,851	87.2%	$251,901	87.0%	$6,872	7.9%	$41,115	14.2%
Aug-04	89,524	$298,654	77,796	86.9%	$261,322	87.5%	$7,162	8.0%	$41,513	13.9%
Sep-04	92,458	$311,897	80,069	86.6%	$270,103	86.6%	$7,027	7.6%	$39,923	12.8%
Oct-04	97,114	$318,694	84,004	86.5%	$276,626	86.8%	$7,478	7.7%	$40,155	12.6%
Nov-04	99,365	$322,145	85,851	86.4%	$283,488	88.0%	$7,651	7.7%	$39,302	12.2%

Review

Once scorecards are built and implemented, a postimplementation review is a good way to identify gaps or shortcomings in the overall scorecard development and implementation process, and conversely, to recognize areas of effectiveness. This serves to make subsequent scorecard development projects more efficient and effective. The review should be done with all parties involved, as detailed in Chapter 2.

Some key questions that should be covered are:

- Was data cleansing required? If it was, logic for the cleansing should be stored.
- Was the interviewing process with, for example, adjudicators and collectors, successful in identifying predictive variables and changes in characteristics across time? This process should then be repeated for future projects. In cases where the scorecard development analyses proved that the information given by the interviewees may not have been correct, such information should be passed back to the adjudicators, for example, so that they can adjust their expectations. For example, adjudicators may have thought that young people living in urban centers were high-risk because they had high rents and moved jobs as well as homes frequently, but analysis showed that they were good risks because those are considered "normal" behavior in urban centers. In most cases, the results of interactive grouping can be presented to those responsible for adjudication or portfolio management, since the information is fairly intuitive, visual, and easily understood. It can also lead to improved risk management through a better understanding of the risk factors affecting your portfolio.
- Were there any specific elements that made your portfolio unique, such as seasonality or periods of abnormal activity? If so, such information should be documented for future development as well as portfolio reviews.
- Were there any occasions when the project stood still? Could something be done in the future to avoid such occurrences? These include waiting for data, inability to interpret results or data, fail-

ure of other departments to do their part due to bad planning, not being able to implement the scorecard, inability to agree on a cut-off or other strategy, and so forth.

- Was there any "data tricks" or transformation of data that made the job of scorecard development easier?

- Were there any data elements that caused problems?

- Were there any surprises or unintended consequences once strategy was developed and implemented? Was this a communications issue (i.e., those affected did not know) or was it a failure to forecast? If so, more "what if" type analysis should be done.

- Was the reporting implemented before the scorecard?

Most of these questions—and their answers—have been covered in the book. Nevertheless, mistakes often get made. The important thing, however, is to learn from them and to ensure that each successive scorecard development project gets more efficient, better organized, and—above all—more intelligent.

Bibliography

Basel Committee on Banking Supervision. 2003. *Quantitative Impact Study 3.* Basel: Bank for International Settlements.

Basel Committee on Banking Supervision. 2004. *International Convergence of Capital Measurement and Capital Standards: A Revised Framework.* Basel: Bank for International Settlements.

Hand, D.J. 2000. "Reject Inference in Credit Operations: Theory and Methods." In *Handbook of Credit Scoring*, ed. Elizabeth Mays. New York: Routledge 2000.

Hand, D.J., and W.E. Henley. "Can Reject Inference Ever Work?" *IMA Journal of Mathematics Applied in Business and Industry* 5 (1993): 45–55.

Hsia, David. "Credit Scoring and the Equal Credit Opportunity Act." *Hastings Law Journal* 30, no. 2 (November 1978): 371–448.

Joanes, D.N. "Reject Inference Applied to Logistic Regression for Credit Scoring." *IMA Journal of Mathematics Applied in Business and Industry* 5 (1993/4): 35–43.

Mays, E., ed. 1998. *Credit Risk Modeling.* Chicago: Glenlake Publishing.

Potts, W.J.E., M.J. Patetta. 2000. *Predictive Modeling Using Logistic Regression: Course Notes.* Cary, NC: SAS Institute.

Rud, O.P. 2001. *Data Mining Cookbook.* Hoboken, NJ: John Wiley & Sons.

Index